VOLUME I

Christian Social Responsibility

A SYMPOSIUM IN THREE VOLUMES

EXISTENCE TODAY

Edited by

HAROLD C. LETTS

Director for Social Action, Board of Social Missions,
The United Lutheran Church in America

MUHLENBERG PRESS   **PHILADELPHIA**

December 1958

Preface

Christian churches in the twentieth century have witnessed two world-wide wars. They have seen in the emergence of Communism and Nazism shocking testimony that Western society is deeply secularized and alienated from its Christian roots. At the same time, churches have become aware that they have been living too much in isolation. They have found themselves unable to speak clearly and pertinently to this crisis in culture.

This has led the churches to rethink their mission, and to organize efforts to minister more effectively to the whole life of society. The organization and program of the World Council of Churches is, in part, an example of these efforts. Churches in many lands have undertaken activities to reach out to the laity and even to confer with those outside the life of the church so that the church may know the burdens men carry and how the church can help.

Within the United Lutheran Church in America, this desire to minister more fully to all men was evident in the first postwar report of President Franklin Clark Fry to the 1946 convention and in the resultant establishment of a Commission on Faith and Life. That commission in 1948 recommended that the Board of Social Missions make

A scholarly study, which may eventuate in a definitive book, of the Lutheran approach to Christian social responsibility. This book should bring together and clarify the full teachings of Scripture on this subject, the witness of our confessions thereto, and all the pertinent pronouncements of the U.L.C.A. Its chief purpose would be to school Lutherans in the Scriptural and confessional grounds for social action. A study book growing out of this definitive study would be desirable for use by laymen.

This recommendation led to the writing of this book. It represents an effort by fourteen pastors, church executives, and theological professors to clarify and restate the evangelical view of social responsibility. This group has met regularly during the past six years. All of the chapters have been reviewed and redrafted in the light of extensive discussion. While we are not in full agreement on all points, nevertheless, the result represents a very substantial measure of agreement. This book is actually the product of group study, though each author wishes to take full responsibility for the views presented in his chapter.

The members of the Board of Social Missions have reviewed and made suggestions about the chapters and submit this book to the United Lutheran Church in America in fulfilment of the responsibility laid upon them by the 16th biennial convention.

During this six-year study, the editor and the authors have been assisted by many people. Especially deserving of mention are:

Dr. E. E. Flack	Dr. Sten Rodhe
Dr. C. Franklin Koch	Dr. Carl C. Rasmussen
Dr. Harold H. Lentz	Dr. John Schmidt
Dr. Bertha Paulssen	Dr. Russell D. Snyder

The authors are grateful for the careful attention to the preparation and typing of the manuscripts given by Miss Dorothy E. Pfister. The editor acknowledges with appreciation the kindness of the publishers of works mentioned in the footnotes in granting permission to quote from their publications. Finally, the editor wishes to express his gratitude to the writers who have joined him in this study. They have shared their faith with him and have immeasurably strengthened him for the work to which he is called.

HAROLD C. LETTS, EDITOR

Lutheran Church House
New York City
December 21, 1956

Preface to Volume I

Christian Social Responsibility is being published in three separately bound volumes. This first volume is subtitled "Existence Today."

In Volume II, entitled "The Lutheran Heritage," the specific historical influences which have led the Lutheran church to its present deep concern about social responsibility are outlined.

In Volume III, "Life in Community," there is a full discussion of the ethical structure on which all effective Christian social action must be built. Relationships of Christian faith to culture, economic life, political order, and family life are discussed.

Tables of contents for Volumes II and III appear on the inside back of this volume.

Contents

VOLUME I—EXISTENCE TODAY

EXISTENCE TODAY

CHAPTER I

Western Society in Transformation

by Karl H. Hertz

In the ninth book of *The Republic* Plato speaks of the terror that may come to a man in his dreams. In a passage that foreshadows Freud, he describes how in sleep "the wild beast within us, gorged with meat and drink, starts up and having shaken off sleep, goes forth to satisfy his desires." The words of Plato have an interest for us beyond the historical because he, too, was writing in the midst of a society in travail, and in *The Republic*, in a language rich in detail and poignant with the memories of his own experiences, Plato recorded the decline of Athens from a society ruled by honor through plutocracy and democracy to the depths of tyranny.

Plato wrote as a prophet as well as a philosopher. With premonitory zeal he looked upon the turmoil which a century of commercial expansion and imperialistic growth had brought to the world he knew, and set down both an epitaph for what had gone before and a dream of what should be.

We in our day have done likewise. Two such dreams, in the form of Utopian novels, may well fix the limits for the problem discussed in this chapter. The first, analogous to Plato's philosopher's kingdom, is Edward Bellamy's *Looking Backward* (1887). Starting with a strong moral reaction to the waste and corruption of an industrial civilization, in which greed served as a first principle, Bellamy drew up the blueprints of a society in which

3

philosophers indeed might easily be kings. But more recently Western man has had another dream, one not unlike the last stages of the Platonic decline of the city. George Orwell's *Nineteen Eighty-Four* (1949), perhaps best called a counter-Utopian novel, stands as the answer of the mid-twentieth century to the dreams of the late nineteenth, as a nightmare in which we subconsciously experience the horror of approaching catastrophe.

The change of mood from *Looking Backward* to *Nineteen Eighty-Four* measures the depth of the fall of Western man, from proud self-assurance in the inevitability of progress (whether through capitalism or socialism) to terrified anticipation of the imminence of disaster.[1] This change of mood with its attendant terror about the future defines the predicament which we must face in our day. Perhaps the issue can be stated thus. Bellamy, standing at an early vantage point in the history of industrial society and trusting in the dream, looked ahead and prophesied the coming of Utopia. Orwell, standing at a later point, has experienced the nightmare and sees in it the abomination of desolation.

Our first duty is not the taking of sides. We must rather inquire after causes; we must probe behind the symptoms of the nightmare to the facts of social structure, for our sense of catastrophe is a disguised confession that deep-seated flaws exist in the civilization of the West.

Simply stated, the basic social structure of the West has been transformed by the process of *industrialization; collectivism* is more and more becoming the dominant form of social organization. Implicit in these changes is the threat of *totalitarianism*.

It is essential from the very beginning to grasp the difference between our kind of society and the kind of society which we

[1] Documented in our day by Hannah Arendt, *The Origins of Totalitarianism* (New York: Harcourt, Brace and Co., 1951), which accepts the coming terror with a kind of existentialist resignation. Cf. Philip Rieff, "The Theology of Politics: Reflections on Totalitarianism as the Burden of Our Time," *Journal of Religion*, XXXII (1952), 119-126.

will find in most other parts of the world. For the civilization that characterizes Western Europe and America and the Westernized portions of the rest of the globe differs strikingly not only from its Oriental contemporaries but also from most of its predecessors. As we list some of its characteristics we shall begin to discover the form which our problems take.

Western society is urbanized and industrialized with a highly developed and complex system of communication (including a generally high literacy rate). Its basic economic form has been that of a capitalistic market economy. Its predominant political form has tended to be democratic. Technology has played an important role as the handmaiden of the above developments and provides the instruments without which neither industry nor commerce could function, neither city nor democratic state on any large scale survive. Finally, the basic values which Western man holds dear have tended to be secular, scientific, rational, and progressive. It must be conceded that some of these traits have appeared elsewhere, but nowhere have they been so highly developed as in the West. Elsewhere social organization tends to be most frequently in terms of village economies and market towns with agriculture (less frequently, fishing) the predominant form of economic activity; limited communication (including much illiteracy), limited participation in government, and lack of technological development are major traits. Tradition is more important than reason, and in general the masses are resigned to the unchanging evil of the world.

The above contrast is, of course, both too simply and too sharply drawn. Still the essential truth remains: Western society is a different kind of society from its contemporaries.[2]

A second point, equally important for our understanding of the problem, is that Western society was itself once traditional, agri-

[2] Sociologists will recognize the distinction between the *gemeinschaftlich* (communal, folk) and the *gesellschaftlich* (associational, urban) types of social organization. The original source is Ferdinand Tönnies, *Gemeinschaft*

cultural, and village-centered. By a series of changes over a period of many centuries a transformation has occurred in the life of Western society which is far-reaching and nowhere completely measurable. Changes have not, of course, occurred in a universally uniform way. Rather, they have taken place at different rates in different places and at different times. The transition is nowhere complete. No clear picture of the form which the social order of the West will take in the next stage of its development yet exists.

We can now briefly list the major changes by means of which the new kind of Western society arose. First, the Industrial Revolution, the basic change in the instruments and organization of production which provided the economic foundation of the West. Second, the demographic revolution, the upsurge in population from which came the working force for the factories of Europe and the swarm of immigrants who settled the centers of Western society outside Europe itself. Third, urbanization, a product of the preceding yet important enough to merit separate mention. Fourth, the revolution in transportation and communication of which the growth in literacy of Western man is a part. Fifth, the political revolution, the rise of democracy and representative systems of government and the increasing importance of public opinion. Sixth, the religious revolution, including not only the Protestant Reformation and the Roman Counter Reformation, but also the continuing religious reorientation of Western man, of which the Enlightenment is a symbol. Seventh, the educational revolution, the rise of public schools, the replacement of tradition by science as a source of knowledge and the increasing dependence on contemporaries for norms rather than on prede-

und Gesellschaft, trans. by C. P. Loomis as *Fundamental Concepts of Sociology* (New York: American Book Co., 1940).

More exactly, the relevant contrast is not between urban and primitive, but between urban and peasant, the latter a more complex traditional type supporting at times a highly sophisticated and urbane ruling class.

cessors.[3] Eighth, an accompanying change in the structure of the family.

THE INDUSTRIAL REVOLUTION

At least three kinds of economic change can be detected in the revolutionary upheavals of the sixteenth and seventeenth centuries in which the modern world received its beginning. The industrial revolutions (there was more than one) were in part the successors of agricultural and mercantile revolutions. Thus the breakup of the feudal world saw an agricultural revolution, marked by numerous peasant uprisings, which increased the efficiency of agricultural production sufficiently to make available both a surplus to feed the populations of the rising towns, and a supply of labor for the new mines and factories. At the same time a mercantile revolution took place, mercantile ventures were founded, banking developed, and trade, especially foreign trade, grew in importance. Surpluses without markets were worthless; markets without commodities, meaningless. Together they spelled a new kind of economic system.

In this economic development the Industrial Revolution was the third phase. For surplus population and surplus food made possible the development of nonagricultural production. At the same time a market was available for the sale of the products of mine and factory. While the causes of the Industrial Revolution and its historic development are much more complex than this sketch indicates, the interdependence of agricultural, mercantile, and industrial revolutions should be clear enough. Most important, however, is the transformation of the social order which accompanied these revolutions. As the assembly line replaced the ox-drawn plow, as the peasant village gave way to the crowded metropolis, the old social order was shattered and a new organization began to take shape on its ruins.

[3] The last three changes mentioned will not be treated in detail in this chapter, since they will be carefully scrutinized in the chapters immediately following.

As we explore some of the salient features of this transformation, we may quite logically begin with the market. For it was to the market that the farmers and craftsmen brought their surpluses. The modern market, however, differs radically from the market which the medieval peasant knew. His market was truly a market place, a specific local center where he did what little trading he could afford. Today's market is a million places—it is, in fact, the entire world. More accurately, for many commodities there is a single world market and a single world price. Thus did the economic revolution of the West transform the local markets of the medieval world.

Not only did the new market burst the bonds of the peasant community, but it also transformed the rules of exchange most radically. For the old economic order was essentially self-sufficient, and the basic economic functions of production, distribution, and consumption were carried on in small groups bound together by traditional ties. The allotment of tasks and rewards in the feudal economy was often determined by "the custom of the manor," by personal relationships, and by considerations of military and political fealty. No purely economic buyer-seller relationship existed, for example, between lord and villein. The tie between men was personal. But in the new economy price, determined by the automatic interplay of supply and demand, was the arbiter of values. Distribution was the impersonal function of the market; producers set their tasks by their expectations of what the market would bring; consumers bought goods when the prices were acceptable.

Distribution was thus severed from production and consumption, and a whole series of distributive institutions developed (commodity exchanges, wholesalers, brokers, commercial bankers, to name a few). Thus the middleman, himself not a producer but a manipulator of commodities, the object of resentment both to producers (cf. the history of agrarian revolt) and consumers, came to play a predominant role in society. In economic language, exchange value became more important than use values. All these new institutions operated according to a rationally calculated system of balancing profits and losses, in which all commodities were reduced to the common denominator of prices. The rules of the market were both rational and universal.

The new economy had another characteristic that did not become immediately apparent. It was inherently dynamic; in fact, it constantly revolutionized itself. John Locke had already surmised that, with the introduction of money, many of the old limits on accumulation no longer held.[4] A commodity can be bought and sold many times; often it can be used only once. Thus, for example, the number of bushels of wheat *traded* on a commodity exchange may exceed by many times the number of bushels actually *consumed* in the economy. The introduction of money thus has revolutionary effects in the market.

Equally revolutionary effects are apparent in the sphere of competition. The struggle for profits is a struggle for markets, for larger output, or lower cost, i.e., it is a struggle in which the conditions of production are subject to ceaseless change and one in which technological change is almost the *sine qua non* of continued economic survival. Even the successful monopolist must constantly be on his guard against competition from a new commodity, a new technological discovery, a new source of supply, or even a new form of business organization. Therefore, he must fear not only competition which strikes at his profits, but even competition which threatens his very existence.[5] Capi-

---

[4] *Second Essay of Civil Government*, chap. V, "Of Property."

[5] Joseph A. Schumpeter, *Capitalism, Socialism, and Democracy* (New York: Harper & Bros., 1942), p. 84. Examples abound: the invention of the automobile, the introduction of plastics—in our day, the atomic revolution.

Given the harsh condition of survival of classical laissez faire, it is small wonder that as soon as possible businessmen attempted to insure more "orderly" conditions in the market and to protect themselves from the dangers of unrestricted competition. For documentation see George W. Stocking and Myron W. Watkins, *Cartels in Action* (New York: Twentieth Century Fund, 1946). A more cynical view of the same subject can be

talism thus constantly destroys its old forms and creates new ones in order to survive. Ceaseless change is part of its law of survival.

Thus, the small workshop of the individual craftsmen yielded to the factory system and, in the twentieth century, to mass production. Mechanized mass production, symbolized by the assembly line, is the predominant trait of modern industrial society. Small factories and medium-sized ones still exist, even in considerable numbers, but the tone and tempo of production is set by the large mass production unit. By the same token the assembly line determines the relationship of the worker to his job. In the mechanized world of the factory, the worker is a cog, almost automatic (except for his human frailties which make him less efficient than the machine he operates), standardized, impersonal, replaceable within a minimum time. The American production record in World War II illustrates clearly the nature of the mass production worker. During that war Willow Run could sustain a labor turnover equivalent to a new labor force every ten months and yet bombers were turned out and, in fact, production rose almost to the very end.[6] Housewives were transformed into production workers, and still the exceedingly complex machines of modern warfare flowed in large quantities from the assembly lines. Using slave labor and peasants forcibly converted into industrial workers, the Germans and the Russians achieved similar "miracles" of production.

As the factory system developed, the number of tasks performed in the productive process multiplied many times. Thus arose the modern division of labor in which the majority of men

found in Thurman Arnold, *The Folklore of Capitalism* (New Haven: Yale Univ. Press, 1937).

[6] L. J. Carr and J. E. Stermer, *Willow Run* (New York: Harper & Bros., 1952). In the 31 months period from Dec. 1, 1941 to June 30, 1944 the bomber plant hired 88,630 men and women to maintain a work force which during the time averaged 29,354 a day. Turnover during 31 months averaged 9.7 per cent a month or 116.7 per cent a year. During an active production life of 43 months, Willow Run used 4.16 workers for every job in the plant.

found that their productive tasks had been reduced to a few operations. "Specialization," as applied to this division of labor is a misleading word, for it implies a selected complex of skills. It is true, of course, that on certain technical levels of production, "specialists," i.e., men with specialized training and skills, are required. But on the assembly line itself the complex operations of the skilled worker are broken down into a series of simple operations assigned to different persons. Skill, the personal nexus between artisan and product, is less necessary than ever before. Thus the modern worker is indeed a replaceable cog. In the final analysis the division of labor has reduced the craftsman to a semi-automaton.[7]

The cabinetmaker, the shoemaker, the leatherworker, to mention a few of the ancient crafts, owned the tools of their trade. But the modern worker brings only himself to his job—neither tools nor product are his. His skills are often limited to tending a machine, and his knowledge of the total productive process to little more than the small part he plays. He is often a man alienated from any sense of workmanship, a man who sees his work not as a vocation, but just as a job. He has in truth, as Marx noted, become a commodity, a thing, not a person.

It becomes therefore eminently worth while to inquire into the motivation of the industrial worker. Despite the fact that the West is now a highly mechanized civilization, Western man did not take kindly and voluntarily to the machine. Some part of the early industrial population indeed was recruited from the apprentices and journeymen of the towns. The greater part, however, came from the surplus agricultural population. They came, in most instances, not because they wanted to, but because they had to. Enclosures, famines, agricultural depressions, and

---

[7] The above exaggerates, of course, but the security of the worker in his job, his protection from economic obsolescence (the seniority principle), is the result of collective action by workers and of political interference, that is, of the contravention of the rules of classical economics.

11

overpopulation forced them into the towns and into the factories.[8] The early economic writings frequently reflect the fact that the discipline of the nascent factory system was almost unbearably harsh. Women and children (as young as eight and nine), as well as men, were driven to work for long hours under barbarous conditions by employers who were not necessarily either sadists at heart or greed-driven monsters. The owners knew no other way to get workers to subject themselves to the implacable tempo of machine production; they justified themselves because they believed that their employees would not work any longer than they were forced to, that only the desperate necessity of survival would persuade them to accept the factory as a place of employment, that only the fear of starvation induced by low wages would keep the workers on the job. "The iron law of wages," as this doctrine was called, was the intellectual version of the disciplinary measures by which the peasant populations of the world were transformed into proletarians. A similar process of iron discipline has characterized the transformation of the peasantry into an industrial and agricultural proletariat (collective farmers) in the Soviet Union. Just as the apologists of nineteenth-century laissez faire referred to the necessary principles of their economic doctrines to rationalize the brutality

[8] England struggled with the depopulation of rural areas, enclosures, and agrarian revolt at the very beginning of the modern period. See R. H. Tawney, *The Agrarian Problem in the Sixteenth Century* (London: Longmans, Green and Co., 1912). As early as 1349 the Statute of Labourers had forbidden indiscriminate almsgiving; thus the mendicants of the Middle Ages could be transformed into wage workers, often with little improvement in the physical conditions of life. On the market economy and its relation to the English poor, see Karl Polanyi, *The Great Transformation* (New York: Farrar and Rinehart, Inc., 1944). For a systematic study of the problem of motivation, see Wilbur E. Moore, *Industrialization and Labor* (Ithaca: Cornell Univ. Press, 1951).

The problem was not one of the rural population alone. The apprentices of seventeenth-century London found themselves engaged in a losing struggle against the incipient capitalism of the leading guildmasters of the time. Despite protests and participation in the political action of the Puritan Revolution, many of them were transformed from potential masters into industrial wage-workers.

of the factory and argued that without discipline all would be lost, so the slave-masters of the Soviet justify their Five Year Plans by appeal to the necessary principles of Marxian economics. In both instances industrialization proceeds at highly accelerated rates. The truth behind the images of worker resistance, whether in terms of inherent improvidence (capitalism) or the persistence of a bourgeois mentality (the Soviets) is that, until a reorientation of motives occurs, rural populations will not seek industrial employment with any eagerness. Only the breakdown of the rural economy, the pressure of poverty and hunger, or the application of political coercion has forced them to give up the security of their customary ways for the factory and the industrial city.[9]

Even after the transformation of the peasant into the industrial worker, it remains a fact that attitudes toward the job and motivations for effort differ widely between the front office and the assembly line. To the manager the logic of profits is convincing. The lowering of production costs seems inherently rational. To the worker any increase in individual productivity ("the speed-up") often appears as a very specific threat to his job. His first loyalty is to his fellow workers, not to the system, particularly not to its managers.

It is at this point that labor organizations play the most important role. For the trade union, as the European recognized long before the American, is not simply an association for the economic protection of the worker. Written into the charters of the labor movements from the very beginning is concern for the dignity of labor. In the modern industrial system work has lost its meaning for many men; the semi-automaton of the assembly line may hardly be said to have a vocation. Into the vacuum left by the dissolution of kinship ties and the traditional institutions of the peasant village, as well as by the general failure of organized

[9] Thus, "studies of factory labor recruitment in India uniformly testify to the significant role of abject poverty, periodic threat of famine, and endemic starvation in pushing workers out of rural villages into other employments." Moore, *op. cit.*, p. 50.

religion to deal with industrial society, the labor organization moved as a new institutional form to meet the new conditions of life. It offered the worker security and dignity, a sense of belonging and a new comradeship of equals. (Some American unions are still known as Brotherhoods.) Like the church the older unions in particular had ladies' auxiliaries and youth groups, sponsored social evenings, picnics, and dances. Today the union offers the worker personal counseling, education and recreation, economic advice, and welfare services.[10]

The working class is not the only product of industrial society. Capitalism has revolutionized the middle class as well and brought into existence a new middle class, the white collar worker. If independence, whether as a small businessman or as a free professional, was the mark of the old middle class, dependence on others through salaried employment is the mark of the new. It includes the armies of office workers which modern industry and government demand, the battalions of salespeople who work in the department stores, the squads of junior executives on the staffs of modern corporations, the research workers, the social scientists, and the accountants who make their living by selling their brain power to the corporate giants of our economy. These are the nameless little people who dream of independence, who are too proud to join a trade union. Consequently they often earn less than the skilled blue collar worker and are constantly beset by the insecurity of a limited income, the frustration of the struggle for status that never quite succeeds, the disillusionment with the power of "the common man" to mold his own future.[11]

[10] In Europe even more than in America the trade union defines the world of the industrial worker. For the expansion of institutional services on the part of labor one need only note as examples the work of the Amalgamated Clothing Workers, the International Ladies' Garment Union, or the CIO Community Services Councils.

[11] For a full discussion of the significance of the new middle class see C. Wright Mills, *White Collar* (New York: Oxford Univ. Press, 1951). Very interestingly the reference to the "common man" in our day tends to be associated with intolerant rather than with democratic attitudes. It is

A look at what has happened to the owner of "private property," the solid symbol of the old middle class, perhaps best illustrates the predicament of the middle classes, old and new. For in the twentieth century ownership has undergone an amazing diffusion (one American corporation claims over a million stockholders) and an equally amazing dilution. For if the worker has been separated from his tools, the owner has lost contact with his property. Private ownership in a farm every acre of which one has tended or in a store whose counters and stockroom are one's daily surroundings is one thing; a stock certificate for twenty shares of U.S. Steel is surely another. What is involved is not merely the loss of control over one's property; equally important is the disappearance of tangibility. The owner often knows as little about the product he is financing as the worker on the assembly line does about what he is fabricating. Ownership in our day is, for the most part, a matter of paper claims to machines and buildings the owner may never have set eyes on. It is a stock quotation in one's daily paper, a dividend check received quarterly. It is a monetary abstraction—and it is just as exchangeable a cog on the financial assembly line as the worker is on the factory assembly line.

The effects on the social status of owners is exceedingly important. To be an owner, especially of a workshop or a trading establishment, was at one time a matter of considerable pride. For such ownership of "the means of production" gave one standing as a member of the bourgeoisie. Such a person was a solid, substantial citizen of the community—a person who counted and one whose decisions carried weight. For ownership had a meaningful function, and that function gave security and status. But with the loss of contact with the productive process, with

"an expression of the rejection of personal involvement in politics," bearing "none of the equality of self-assertiveness associated with earlier democratic ideology." Bruno Bettelheim and Morris Janowitz, *Dynamics of Prejudice* (New York: Harper & Bros., 1950), p. 93. Cf. also Leo Lowenthal and Norbert Guterman, *Prophets of Deceit* (New York: Harper & Bros., 1950).

15

the separation of the owner from his property, function has disappeared. Or rather, the owner is no longer a producer, but simply a supplier of capital, one who puts up the money which others put to work in the productive process.

Here, too, we need to see that institutions have changed along with economic forms. In the small city the community of interests among owners found its organized outlet in common participation in churches, lodges, service clubs, and a variety of other voluntary associations. Thus owners could meet with one another, and through their organizations exercise the power that went with their status in the community. These organizations helped create and express the bourgeois consensus of opinion. By membership in them "the people who counted" could mold the life of their communities. In the metropolis, however, most of these organizations have deteriorated; for the small entrepreneur (e.g. the owner of a "hole-in-the-wall" grocery store) there exists no effective common organizational meeting ground with "the people who count," the upper coterie of industrialists, bankers, and so forth, who make the important decisions. The owner is cut off from below by his antipathy to labor; from above, by lack of effective channels of interaction. He is "in the middle"; clinging to unreal economic ideas, he is bewildered by the actualities of economic life.[12]

This very loss of status and power, it may at least be hypothesized, makes small owners receptive to fascist propaganda. For it is a familiar theme in the press that "labor," especially "the labor bosses," must be responsible for the loss of function of ownership. Labor has indeed limited some of the powers of corporate management, but it is the sheerest fiction that the average stockholder in an American corporation ever exercises these functions, except vicariously. Nevertheless, insecurity of status breeds a demand for retribution. Should the small businessman suffer the same

[12] Cf. C. Wright Mills, "The Middle Classes in Middle-Sized Cities," *American Sociological Review*, X (1945), 242-249, and *White Collar, op. cit.*

radical loss of investments through inflation or economic collapse that the German middle classes suffered in the 1920's, one may guess that he, too, will follow the would-be Führers into the austere Utopia of totalitarianism.[13]

The chief motive of modern owners thus seems to be security rather than profit. They are not the risk-takers of the free enterprise system, but the *rentiers*, investors looking for a secure income and not seeking venturesomely after a new outlet for capital. An anonymous multitude (by no means all of them widows and orphans), they look to the system to preserve their privileges; therefore politically many of them still accept the outworn shibboleths of an economic system that no longer exists. Ownership itself is becoming increasingly collectivized and indirect, removed from the realm of individual decision and individual possession. To be an "owner" is to be a small cog in a complexly-structured hierarchy of economic relations, and in this relational structure only those near the top of the organizational pyramid can exercise effective power. Ownership is thus a collective affair, carried out by agents on behalf of the individuals concerned without any individual knowledge or interest for the most part. A large share of the capital investments made by American "owners" are made for them indirectly by the insurance companies in which they hold policies. Nor is this the only form of the collectivization of investments, for one of the most popular advertising appeals to the contemporary investor is that of the investment pool or mutual fund.[14] The investor no longer buys stock in a corporation

[13] Evidence that loss in status is accompanied by a rise in fascist attitudes may be found in Bettelheim and Janowitz, *Dynamics of Prejudice, op. cit.* An exploration of fascist-minded personalities is reported in T. W. Adorno, *et al., The Authoritarian Personality* (New York: Harper & Bros., 1949).

[14] "The investor himself has made it unmistakably clear that he is not interested in ownership; indeed, that he does not want it. He has abdicated his legal right of control and he resists all attempts on the part of management to make him take an interest in the enterprise, let alone participate in its affairs." Peter F. Drucker, *The New Society: The Anatomy of the Industrial Order* (New York: Harper & Bros., 1949).

directly; he pools his money with that of other investors, and the managers of the investment pool or mutual fund then buy a diversified range of stocks for him. Thus ownership in our corporate economy has been emptied almost completely of its traditional content. For better or worse, investment has been privately collectivized.

As the transformation of ownership has proceeded, the old function of control has come into new hands, that of the managers or executives. The power of management still rests, in the final analysis, on the legal structure of the property system, but today that property is corporate rather than individual. Legally, too, the managers remain responsible to the owners who have only delegated their powers to management. Actually, through the proxy system and other devices, minority and management control is the rule in the larger corporations. Thus the managers enjoy a high degree of irresponsible social power.[15] Using the corporate structure as a base, while still giving voice to the old shibboleths of free enterprise, the managers could presumably act as the carriers of even more revolutionary changes than have thus far occurred.[16]

This revolution will be tempered by the fact that most of the careers of "top management" are still linked inextricably with the property system they administer. Management, in fact, is the new profession for enterprising young men just out of college, just as entrepreneurship was the high road to success in the past. The rationalization of business enterprise has grown apace, and the

[15] A. A. Berle and Gardner Means, *The Modern Corporation and Private Property* (New York: Macmillan Co., 1934) is the almost classic work. Drucker, *op. cit.*, pp. 340-341, picks up where Berle and Means left off and spells out the socio-economic implications of the new forms in thought-provoking detail. "The best solution," he feels, "would be simply to legalize the de facto situation. The investor in the large enterprise should not require any legal title of ownership, but only a claim to economic rewards."

[16] James Burnham, *The Managerial Revolution* (New York: John Day Co., 1940) exaggerates the power of the managers by overlooking the manager's stake in property institutions and the differences in political and cultural traditions in different societies.

manager today is an officeholder in a hierarchy of officeholders; he starts on his career as a junior executive, as an administrative assistant, or as a lesser supervisor, and over the years, either within the same company or by transfer to a larger company, works his way up to greater things. He is, in fact, a part of the vast impersonal bureaucracy of the corporate world. If the pace is hard, the privileges are many (an expense account, secretarial help, club memberships), and advancement a fairly assured prospect.

If the manager's position is in some respects analogous to that of the civil service bureaucrat, an important difference still remains. For the rules of success for the industrial manager are still ultimately formed by the vicissitudes of the market. In fact, his daily routine is a part of the battle for production, the struggle for sales, the everlasting conquest of the market which is indigenous to capitalism. Thus the manager's stake in capitalism is real. The managers may indeed control the corporations, but the rules of corporate success still dominate the managers. A "managerial revolution," therefore, will remain a struggle for the protection of the economic powers of corporate capitalism. Although the managers may come to terms with the agitators of the right in the political arena, there is no inherently necessary connection between them and the totalitarian politicians. The predominant interest of the industrial manager presumably remains economic rather than political.

The typical social structure in which the manager functions is the corporation. The corporation is, in fact, the sociological embodiment of the revolution by which our society has been transformed.[17] As an economic structure, the corporation was, of course, necessary for the expansion to the vast scale of operation which characterizes Western capitalism. For it was through

[17] It is interesting to note that neither the Communist nor the Socialist intends to abolish the corporate form of social organization; they only intend to take over its management.

the corporation that the co-ordination of production in the assembly lines of modern factories was made possible. The inherent dynamics of the market economy, moreover, resulted in a constant increase in the size of corporations and in the constant concentration of economic power.

The consequences of this change are many. The corporation has now become an almost autonomous sociological entity with its own laws of survival and its own inherent dynamism.[18] The inner structure of the corporation, increasingly rationalized in the interests of greater competitive efficiency, has become progressively more bureaucratic, with all the intra-office tensions, breakdowns in communication, red tape and paper work, and informal "political" organization that accompany this change. Its external relationships have also changed: "the invisible hand," by which classical economics deified the practices of the market has given place to "the glad hand," the symbol of that complex of manipulative skills called public relations by which corporations struggle for their proper share of the market.[19] A kind of corporate "sphere of influence" also comes into being. Intracorporate organizations (recreation, welfare, education) arise to supplement and sometimes to supplant those of the political community.[20] The extracorporate sphere includes a whole array of dependent businesses as part of the organization of production, an increasingly large number of dependent retailers for whom the corporation supplies financing, advertising, staff training, and other services. The new economic order is thus a phenomenon of overwhelming sociological and political importance.

The old issue of monopoly is given a changed meaning in this

[18] Cf. especially Drucker, *op. cit.*

[19] The phrase is from David Riesman, *et al., The Lonely Crowd* (Anchor Book; New York: Doubleday & Co., 1953), Chapter VI.

[20] Even religion is not untouched; cf. the developing field of the industrial chaplaincy, a trend which must be separated from the kind of captive subsidized "mill churches" described by Liston Pope, *Millhands and Preachers* (New Haven: Yale Univ. Press, 1942).

new economic setting. For while the crux of the issue of monopoly is always whether or not the monopolist has obtained undue control over the market, the problem of the stability of the market is such a critical one that the uncontrolled market of "old-fashioned capitalism" would no longer be the unmixed blessing that the folklore suggests. We must recognize, above all, that monopoly is not primarily a matter of size. Because of the inherent dynamism of capitalism, even the largest corporation may face a constant threat of competition—the competition of new products, of technological innovation, of new manufacturing processes. Thus to maintain his position, the monopolist may, in the manner of some European capitalists, seek to restrain the introduction of new inventions, to stabilize markets by cartel agreements. The monopolist may forestall competition in another manner, however, by being himself the chief innovator, introducing new products and sponsoring technological development. In either case the practices resorted to represent efforts to deal with the uncertainties of a dynamic economic system in order to introduce an element of stability.

A further aspect of the issue of monopoly power, as Harvard economist John Galbraith has recently pointed out,[21] is that the big firms almost necessarily call big opponents into being. Big buyers, like Sears, Roebuck and Company, confront big sellers; big labor organizations, like the new industrial unions, confront big industry. Between them they create both a competitive situation and a certain degree of economic stability.

It must be kept in mind that not all of the above developments are manifestly against the public interest. Under some circumstances regulation of production (given a small number of firms), division of the market, planned introduction of technological innovations, all of them safeguarding the positions of the partic-

[21] *American Capitalism: The Concept of Countervailing Power* (Boston: Houghton Mifflin Co., 1952).

ipating firms, may seem preferable to the boom and bust associated with the older capitalism in the public mind.[22]

These developments are equivalent to economic planning, and thus our discussion has reached one of the major areas of current economic controversy. Actually the controversy no longer rages over whether there shall be planning. A stable economy requires all the prudent preparation for the future that is possible. The primary questions are those of determining who the planners shall be, what methods of planning shall be used, and where the locus of authority over the planning process shall reside.[23]

In either case, however, the exercise of control over the market is much more than an economic matter. The "organizational revolution" of our day has, in fact, led to an inevitable politicalization of economic life. The struggle for success within the structure of an organization, whether it be a business hierarchy, a trade union bureaucracy, or any other kind of large scale organization, is obviously a political struggle. But the development of the gigantic organizations of our day has forced these giants into an external political struggle, a struggle over labor laws and trade regulations, over international trade agreements and the terms of government contracts, over appropriations for military purchases and the treatment of excess profits, over the

[22] The Schuman Plan integrating the coal-iron-steel industry of Western Europe is an outstanding example. In America the Federal Communications Commission's concern with the problems of color television serves as another example. The "closed shop," as well as the control exercised by some professions over recruitment, are also attempts to stabilize the market. So are such measures as unemployment compensation and deposit insurance. The issue is not stability, but stability on whose behalf?

Trade unions too have participated in these arrangements. Cf. Matthew Josephson, *Sidney Hillman: Statesman of Labor* (New York: Doubleday & Co., 1952). As Philip Taft has pointed out, Hillman was praised for economic practices which in other labor leaders would have been considered "collaborationist." *Commentary*, March, 1953, pp. 312-316. Throughout Hillman's career stabilizing the industry was a major objective of his union policy.

[23] Cf. the excellent book by Robert A. Dahl and Charles E. Lindblom, *Politics, Economics and Welfare* (New York: Harper & Bros., 1953).

control of opinion (public relations) and changes in the individual income tax rate. Business and labor are systems of power, and both realize that political decisions may affect profits and income as drastically as the condition of the market. In fact, some industries might almost be considered "captive corporations" because of the degree to which their profits are dependent on government (particularly military) contracts. Business is no longer just business; it is politics as well.

COLLECTIVISM

The whole issue of the concentration of power, of the attempt of economic interests to stabilize the market, therefore, reflects a more fundamental change in the structure of society. The kind of capitalism which grew out of the breakup of the medieval world and became the typical economic structure of the modern period of history has been transformed. A new industrial society, basically collectivist, whether capitalistic or socialistic in form, is taking its place and giving birth to new issues of power and control.

Before proceeding to the evidence, we need to note a few basic distinctions and definitions. An economy is capitalistic in the classical sense to the extent that ownership and management of capital are vested in private individuals who make economic decisions on the basis of profit and loss. An economy is socialistic to the extent that ownership and management are vested in some public group where decisions are made and risks and rewards shared by some commonly agreed upon rule, which may be the rule of profit and loss. Thus, to prepare for one's old age by personal saving is in the best tradition of classical capitalism; to prepare by participation in a private pension scheme, or to purchase life insurance, especially in a mutual company, is to participate in collective economic action. To participate in Social Security is socialism. To own a Blue Cross policy is, the medical profession notwithstanding, collectivism and, since Blue Cross is nonprofit, a form of socialism.

To substantiate the description of our economy as a form of collectivist capitalism, it is now only necessary to pass in review the evidence already presented in the descriptive paragraphs above. In our economy, private ownership and management have become meaningless, because the owner has been separated from his property. Much ownership is in fact indirect, with insurance companies and investment funds acting as agents for the owners as a group. Private, that is, personal enterprise, is largely limited to the marginal and small scale activities of our economy. Agriculture, through the farm co-operatives, especially in California where agriculture is most commercial, is as much collectivized as industry—and farm prices are no longer set by pure competition. Labor through collective bargaining functions in a similar manner. At all points of our economy collectivism exists.

Collectivism exists, however, without socialism in the traditional sense. It exists in the context of a market system where profit and loss are still meaningful. The crucial question in our economy is, therefore, not collectivism, but the social responsibility of large-scale private collectivism. To whom is a collective enterprise responsible? In neither the large corporation nor the giant trade union is there any effective machinery present to keep the managers responsible to the rank and file—stockholders or workers. By the manipulation of proxies, by the control of the purse, the organs of communication, and the machinery of administration, the perpetuation in power of minorities is not only possible, but actually exists.[24] Here lies the danger point, for since power is concentrated in the hands of a minority at the top, the alliance of these groups could bring into being an organization with far-reaching political consequences. The power of these minorities has been enhanced through the development,

[24] These are illustrations of Robert Michel's "iron law of oligarchy." Cf. his *Political Parties* (Glencoe, Ill.: Free Press, 1949).

particularly by industry, of interest and power groups which are national in extent. Thus trade organizations, national labor organizations, as well as the national organizations of professional groups (American Medical Association, American Bar Association, and so forth) represent systems of power by which a few may, by the manipulation of organizational machinery, control the many to their own purposes.[25]

The possibility of an alliance between the persons who stand at the top of economic organizational pyramids with their counterparts in the political and military structures of society is underlined by the fact that for over a decade the prosperity of business enterprise and the high wages of labor have rested in greater or lesser degree on military expenditures. The cold war has brought into being both in Western Europe and in America a permanent war economy. What would happen to our economic order without "the pump priming" of military purchases is difficult to determine. It is popularly believed that a drastic cut in the military budget would lead to an economic depression.[26] A war economy necessarily means close relationships among the military, the politicians, and the upper leadership of business and labor, for government now becomes the major consumer of many products. The market is thus *politicalized*, not only for commodities but also for labor. In this change the strongly organized have the advantage; the corporate giants, the trade associations, and the powerful trade unions hold strategic positions. Since the

[25] Robert A. Brady, *Business as a System of Power* (New York: Columbia Univ. Press, 1943) discusses one aspect of this problem; C. Wright Mills, *The New Men of Power* (New York: Harcourt, Brace and Co., 1948) speculates on the possibilities of an alliance between sophisticated conservatives, military power, and "realistic" liberals, including labor leaders.

[26] "Pump priming" can of course create prosperity, provided the scale is vast enough, as our war economy shows. If depression resulted from a decrease in military expenditures, further political intervention in the economic system would probably result. Destruction of economic resources is culturally quite permissible when the expenditures are made for military purposes; otherwise, the procedure is called "bureaucratic boondoggling."

politicalization of the economy is at the same time a militarization, the top echelons of the armed forces are also in a position of power. There are advantages for all in an alliance.

TOTALITARIANISM

Such an alliance, despite its threat to the functioning of democracy, would not yet bring totalitarianism. The distinguishing mark of totalitarian societies is the politicalization of all aspects of society. Totalitarianism, whether fascist or communist in form, rejects the priority of economic interests and the freedom of men to pursue individual economic advantage just as it denies the validity of all other nonpolitical interests and suppresses every kind of freedom. Totalitarianism thus draws on more sources in the community than its economic structure; it has its roots in the disturbed personality of modern man, in the romantic deification of the state, and in the deterioration of political morality. To understand the threat of totalitarian power, we must now look at some of the other revolutionary changes in the West that occurred during the period of industrialization.

The economic development of the West was accompanied by a demographic revolution. The population of Western Europe in 1650 was about 100 millions; by 1800 the population of European origin (both inside and outside of Europe) was 200 millions. By 1950 this total, despite declining birth rates, had reached 800 millions.[27]

Population growth is not a peculiarity of the West. In fact, in some respect it is a more acute problem for the East. But a vast difference in the social structure of East and West must also be taken into account. This difference is most apparent in the realm of agriculture, for in the West the increase in population was accompanied by a steady decline in the proportion of persons directly engaged in agriculture. Thus the increased

[27] W. S. and E. S. Woytinsky, *World Population and Production* (New York: Twentieth Century Fund, 1953), pp. 34-36.

population provided more hands to operate machines rather than just more mouths to feed.

It is in the densely populated peasant societies that communism is succeeding. Furthermore, the basic economic program of the Communists in all these lands comprises two points: increasing the efficiency of agriculture through collectivization[28] and industrialization. Communist revolution has not come in the last stages of capitalism but in its earliest stages. The capitalism of the peasant societies, moreover, is not native but imported; the Communists thus have the opportunity to utilize the charges of imperialism and colonialism.

Colonialism and imperialism point out a further problem. As populations expanded on the land, migration set in, first perhaps to the nearest city, then to more distant places. The relative homogeneity of peasant populations gave place to the heterogeneous populations of industrial societies. Both in Europe and America the rural migrant was recruited for the unskilled factory job. In the colonial areas into which the European powers expanded, native peoples were recruited as a labor force for mines and plantations. In the process the traditional ties of the older peasant community or of the native tribe were broken. In many instances, native populations were in fact demoralized. The extent of the damage done depended in part on the cultural difference between the migrant and his host. In this process no one suffered greater hardships than the native peoples of the colonial areas.

This is the heart of the modern race question. Its immediate origin is economic though its effects are cultural and its form is political. For the expanding markets of the West incessantly demanded greater and greater labor power at as low a price as

---

[28] Cf. David Mitrany, *Marx Against the Peasant* (Chapel Hill: Univ. of North Carolina Press, 1950). Tito, too, is struggling with the peasant, for to support his program of industrialization he must secure the surplus agricultural production for the urban market. The peasants, however, are loathe to make the required deliveries.

possible. Thus they engulfed the peasants, whether in the European city or in the American slum, and thus they captured the natives of India and Asia and Africa. The market system destroyed peasant communities, with their traditions and personal loyalties, substituting for them the impersonal cash nexus of the job and the atomistic society of the industrial town or the plantation barracks. Thus the industrial proletariat was born. It was hardly for this reason that the peasant sought the city, yet such by and large was his fate. In America the ceaseless expansion of the economy served to hide the fact, for successive waves of immigrants pushed their predecessors up the status ladder. The older migrant often served as taskmaster for the newcomer. "Race," moreover, served the masters well, for it kept the slum-dweller from realizing the true cause of his condition. At the same time it kept him divided from his natural allies.

To escape from this evil condition, the exploited classes had, for the most part, only one weapon—political organization—including riots, conflicts, and revolution, if these were necessary. Their struggle was twofold, for political rights and for economic equality. In Europe, where class lines were drawn with greater rigidity than in America, the struggle of the proletariat became allied with a much more complete repudiation of established values than in America. Thus Marxism captured the allegiance of vast sections of the working class, and the labor movement developed a political consciousness and an antireligious philosophy which have been foreign to America.[29]

[29] To call "race relations" caste relations conveniently serves to hide their economic basis. "Caste" is a characteristic of some static peasant societies; "race relations" occur in dynamic industrial societies. It is further characteristic of race relations that, like all else in industrial societies, they are subject to constant change. In America where capitalism developed not only at a more rapid pace than elsewhere but also in a frontier situation free from inherited aristocratic structures, "race and minority relations" also took on a different aspect. Not only "the American creed" but also the requirements of the mass market and the assembly line created pressures for equality often surprising to those who still view the American scene from the tradi-

The battleground on which this struggle was fought was the vast industrial metropolis. The very nature of urban life thus also conditioned the form which the struggle took. For the unskilled proletarian from the hinterland, a European peasant village, a Kentucky mountain valley, a folk Negro community in the South, life in the industrial city was a series of crises. Ignorant of the power structure of the community and helpless in the face of the vast impersonal organizations of the metropolis, the only certainties he knew were uncertainties—uncertain employment, inadequate housing, little guarantee of the gratification of the fundamental needs of body and spirit. Troubled over his inability to control his life chances with any degree of success, the slum-dweller sought refuge from his anxieties in a variety of ways. Under the impact of culture shock, having lost his roots in the soil and being unable to strike roots in the pavement, with no sense of belonging, without intimate personal relationships and little security of status, he reacted emotionally rather than rationally. Rationality required resources of leisure and economic security which many did not possess. It was simpler to react to the loss of moral tradition by surrendering to the moral heterogeneity of the city, to the emotional uplift of "holiness" religion, to the physical pleasures of sex and drink, or to the bitter enthusiasm of a fascist political movement. In America, note how the fascist agitator constantly invokes "that old time religion."

Thus we are faced with what Ortega y Gasset has called "the revolt of the masses," the invasion of the barbarians from within. These are the restless settlers of the ultimate frontier—barbarians because they lack a stable cultural tradition to give meaning to their lives, restless because they are participants in a process in which change is the only certainty and tomorrow's problems render yesterday's solutions obsolete. Small wonder that, in their

tional perspective. Nevertheless, in America as elsewhere, equality has not come easily. Bitter political struggles, sometimes marked with violence and still continuing, have marked its course.

bewilderment and insecurity, they are often the easy victims of the hatred-purveying demagogue and hallelujah-shouting storefront revivalist. It is not in this instance lack of education as such or of deliberate evil intent that creates the disorganized, anonymous, anxiety-breeding life of the metropolis. Rather it is the destruction of the old cultural unity of the peasant village together with the lack of an urban cultural tradition. Most men, the truth is, have not yet learned to live in the city. To begin with, the unceasing change in the city environment makes any kind of stable adjustment difficult. Second, under the conditions of urban reproduction, especially as urban centers continue to expand, most city populations are in fact rural populations transformed. Thus the city finds it difficult to achieve cultural stability because in every generation it must assimilate new rural populations. Nevertheless urban traits are the predominant traits of our society. In the final analysis, Western man must learn to live in the city if he expects to survive at all.

The city is thus a paradox, at once the solvent of old loyalties and a creator of the sophisticated rational intellect, the habitat of the urbane. It is by the same token a destroyer of community, breeding anxiety and bewilderment, giving birth to the nameless harried faces that pass at a busy intersection, the human ants that swarm in automobiles bumper to bumper during the rush hours, the impatient throngs that crowd the Sunday highways in a briefly snatched escape from the oppression of the asphalt jungle.

Urban conditions of communication contribute to this invasion of the barbarians from within. The revolution in communications played an important role in the creation of Western society, making it possible to weld together millions in a single community, bringing, through the invention of printing and of the newspaper and its allied technology, a flood of information to the metropolitan masses which even a century ago would have been deemed impossible. Yet the revolution in communications and the accompanying revolution in transportation also played its part in bringing into being the predicament of Western man.

The immense advance in the technology of communication has been accompanied by a vast increase in the size of the communication unit; in truth, the spread of ideas in the Western world is best conceived as the function of "idea industries," whether privately or publicly managed. Ideas are thus standardized and mass-marketed, creating a uniformity of information and of ignorance in vast populations. Thus in the United States, unless the citizen consults some other source of information than his daily paper or the TV newscaster, the man in Portland, Oregon, and the man in Portland, Maine, will probably read or hear the same account. American journalism, it is true, maintains high standards of truthfulness. But even literal veracity can convey misinformation by what it leaves out, by what the newspaper defines as news. The American definition of news is such that the attention of the reader is constantly drawn to the exceptional rather than to the routine. Thus the day-to-day functions of a trade union are not news, but a labor dispute is. Similarly, the 99 per cent plus loyalty record of federal employees is not mentioned but the fractional disloyalty receives columns of attention.

Radio and television, even more than the daily press, also fragmentize the world, as though human history were enacted in fifteen-minute units with regular pauses for the hucksters to deliver their commercials. The fifteen-minute news broadcast and the movie newsreel are, moreover, a kind of surrealist *omnium gatherum* of baseball scores, war news, political second-guessing, crime reporting, human interest filler, and other miscellaneous trifles. Bombarded thus six to a dozen times a day, the citizen can hardly be expected to see life clearly and to see it whole. The performance is much better gauged to arouse his emotions than to stimulate his intellect.

But whether we discuss news or entertainment or education, all of them processes by which we communicate facts and values, traditions and innovations, we confront highly similar situations.

31

Our problem is not one of literacy, not even one of information. We have taught people how to read; we must now teach them how to think. For thinking is much more than the logical manipulation of symbols; it has its own proper virtues which can be acquired only by discipline and practice. The character and integrity of the individual citizen, his commitment to moral values, his willingness to undergo the mental anguish of moral reasoning, his openness of mind to differences of opinion, his patience in debate, his intellectual alertness in the face of demagoguery—these intellectual and moral virtues will provide the strength and vitality necessary for making responsible political decisions. Unless the various institutions of our society which are shaping the character of Western man can produce citizens of this stature, the outlook for ultimate success in the ideological battle will be poor indeed.

THE PREDICAMENT OF DEMOCRATIC GOVERNMENT

In economic collectivism, in the frustrations of urban anonymity, and in the mass emotions of the popular culture, we find fertile ground for the seeds of totalitarian demagoguery. Hatred, insecurity, anxiety, despair—all the ingredients of the witches' brew are ready.

The very fact that in our day men debate the virtues of democracy reminds us of the extent of our predicament. For insecurities in the minds of men both reflect the weaknesses of institutions and contribute to their failure. Paradoxically, moreover, the attack on democratic institutions is launched in the name of "the people." The fascists, whatever their opinion of Anglo-American democracy, never tire of claiming to speak with the authentic voice of "the folk"; the Soviet protagonists proclaim themselves the leaders of "people's democracies."

The political tradition of the West is, in fact, an ambiguous one; the institutional form which political life takes in one country or another is primarily a matter of the particular combination of elements that has occurred. An almost continuous instability has marked the political life of the West since the middle ages, with wide fluctuations between the poles of freedom and tyranny within a single country, e.g., Germany, as well as persistent differences among the various political units themselves. Portugal and Spain, on the one hand, have had predominantly authoritarian institutions; England and America, on the other hand, have had long records of freedom.

To account for these variations, we may postulate certain explanatory hypotheses. First, stable democratic institutions are probably the product of a combination of beliefs, institutional forms, and historical circumstances. Second, their persistence in any community depends in large measure on the existence of certain political habits in the populace. Third, democratic institutions probably flourish best in situations where the other institutions of the community offer them positive support. Our present purpose will not be to attempt to prove these hypotheses, but to use them in order to understand the contemporary political scene, specifically the peril in which democratic institutions find themselves.

Democracy is not instinctive in the mind of man; it must be rooted deeply in the folkways and mores of a people; its practice must become "second nature," a matter of unconscious sentiment and spontaneous allegiance. Democratic institutions do not arise from legislative fiat but by the slow accretion of centuries of institutional growth. For democracy is a complex phenomenon; its "unwritten laws" are as important as its written constitutions; in the American and English tradition it has included a concern for the freedom of men to disagree with authority and an affirmation of the rights of minorities against the majority. The natural-law tradition, especially in America, also contributed a belief in a "higher law" forever beyond the reach of political action. The political rights of men had divine sanction; their governments, however, were held strictly accountable.

33

Governments and politicians, furthermore, enjoyed little prestige in themselves. Even in England, by the segregation of the crown from the political arena, men effectively distinguished between the community to which they owed patriotic duties and the government which they criticized freely and often unmercifully.

Among the institutional forms in which these beliefs received embodiment the two-party system is one of the more important. For the two-party system is an institutionalization of opposition without that kind of ideological separation between parties which characterizes the multi-party systems of the Continent. American parties are, in fact, "unprincipled" coalitions of many interests; even in England the differences between Laborite and Tory are largely matters of degree, not of ideological polarity. Politics has a looseness of structure and an inherent pluralism that allows diversity of opinion and free change of allegiance from election to election.

Long years of historical growth lie behind the development of these beliefs and institutions, years during which the English and the American mind has been shaped into the unconscious practice of democratic habits, e.g., good sportsmanship in accepting election returns; politics as a game in which defeat does not mean suppression but a chance to play again in another election. These and innumerable other facets of democratic political habits, still largely unexplored, probably undergird the great democracies and provide them with their amazing stability.

Finally, we must not overlook the effect of other institutions on the success of democratic political forms. Here we must include the effect of the forms and methods by which internal affairs are conducted. While Machiavelli has always been a major prophet of the diplomatic corps, his followers have had more opportunities than ever before to practice their amoral art in a world in which social change shattered the traditional political communities and revolution and dictatorship apparently made the resort to violence legitimate. There can be no doubt, moreover, that no moral consensus on the methods of statesmanship and no mutual confidence exists among the major powers in the world today. Where distrust reigns, democracy can hardly flourish. In Europe, in addition, the basic institutions of the family, the established churches, the business interests, the entrenched aristocracies, as well as the tradition-bound peasant groups, have in the past almost consistently allied themselves with the antidemocratic parties, if not with the active enemies of democracy. Only in England, in the Dominions, and especially in America, have democratic forms characterized other institutions. In America, pluralism, freedom of association, the lack of entrenched aristocracies, and the freedom of the frontier contributed to a diversity of institutions which provided a fertile soil for democratic forms to flourish.

Anglo-American pluralism is not without its own peculiar temptations of corruption. For the looseness of the associational structure of American life, with its history of limited government, created the conditions under which private economic associations, both of industry and of labor, could grow into private governments at times exercising irresponsible power on a large scale. Under the doctrine of the separation of church and state, itself derived from pluralism, religion became more and more dissociated from the arena in which crucial decisions were reached. The very pluralism of multi-associational society, given the heterogeneity of the immigrant populations that flowed into the industrial centers of America, contributed to the breakdown of community. Thus not even in its religious life was any real identification with the larger life of the community possible.

In America the diversity of religious life accentuated many of these consequences. For, if freedom of religion is the glory of the American church, it is also, though less apparently, the source of one of its greatest dilemmas, especially in the urban community. The diversity of religious associations has often been accompanied by a lack of any genuine religious consensus except in the form of vague and sentimental platitudes. Despite ecumenicity on the national scene and co-operation among religious leaders even in local councils of churches, the average American Protestant goes his own denominational way, altogether too frequently little aware of the larger fellowship of believers. Many an American, too, would be hard put to tell an interviewer the church his neighbor attends or the creed his business associates espouse. Religion has become so private a concern that members of the same household may attend different churches without any particular knowledge either that the differences among them have any religious import or without any conscious effort to practice a genuine ecumenicity. The American middle-class person is, of course, vaguely aware that "religion is a good thing" and that his children profit somehow from attending Sunday school, but he rarely sees any real connection between the church in which he worships and the community in which he makes his living.

Nor should this be surprising. For the successful city church frequently has no direct relationship to any geographical area. The metropolis is its parish, which means that so far as the local concerns of men are involved, the city church has no parish. It is rarely a community church related intimately by history and activity to a circumscribed area. Its parishioners may live anywhere in the city, and may pass three or more churches of the same denomination on their way to Sunday worship. When they arrive they find most of their fellow worshipers to be strangers rather than neighbors. Nor does it matter, for they will not see them again for a week, if they are in church. On the other hand, next-door neighbors may drive off in different directions to church on Sunday morning. Thus effective co-operative Christian action is almost a structural impossibility, and a sense of common participation in the communion of believers almost nonexistent for the laity.

Religious activity has come to mean primarily a one-hour Sunday morning service, and the impact of the church on the community is rendered ineffective in part by the failure of the church to identify itself with the community. The European counterpart of this decline in religious participation arises not from the failure of the church to have a geographical parish, but from its failure to motivate the people in its parish to participate in religious activity. Religious activity has become almost totally irrelevant for the urban man, American and European. No amount of talk about postwar religious revival can gainsay the fact that actual participation in religious life is minimal for the vast majority. The movies, the horse races, even the political candidates on television attract more people and furnish the occasion for more conversations.

The reason for this condition is plain. Politics, economics, and even athletics have more relevance and more impact on the daily existence of the citizen than religion has. They present him with issues with which he must come to terms or they offer him symbols of identification by means of which he is restored for a moment to the status of one who belongs. In its theology the church is a communion or a community; in its practice it is often a gathering of virtual strangers. A closely contested football game will offer its devotees, including clergymen, more of an emotional thrill than the festival of Pentecost. In the anonymous, fragmentary, impersonal life of the industrial cosmopolis, men are seeking for avenues to community. Their deepest needs for intimate relations to their fellows are being frustrated, and consequently they find emotional refuge in "bread and circuses," in athletic frenzies, and in the mass media of entertainment.

In this situation it is small wonder that even the preachers are as much preoccupied with binding up the emotional wounds of the spiritually homeless man as they are with their other parish duties. For the glory of many an urban Protestant pastorate is no longer found in the pulpit, but in the consulting room. Pastoral theology, which once consisted in the art of bringing the consolation of religious doctrine and the sacramental acts of the church to parishioners, has given place to pastoral psychology, the art of bringing "peace of mind" to the despairing, the anxious, and the spiritually defeated. No one can deny the importance of the healing function of the ministry. Yet how often does religious therapy go beyond the individual client, who is a maladjusted person, not a lost soul, and the restoration of his integrity to a genuine restoration of the sense of belonging to the fellowship of believers? The persons whose spiritual wounds have been bound up in the privacy of the pastor's study altogether too often remain strangers in the church on Sunday morning. Meanwhile the pastor moves on to the new appointment of the following week. Pastoral psychiatry may bind up the wounds of the wanderers in the wasteland, but by itself it does not necessarily reach the source of the injury, namely, the loss of the sense of belonging.

The very conditions which an industrial society imposes on its members, its impersonal economic organization, its separation of owners from their property, workers from their tools, its urban heterogeneity and anonymity, its Sunday morning gathering of strangers, limit the resources for security and affection available to the individual to a small circle of persons who constitute his family and perhaps his few intimate friends, persons who in the larger society are caught in the same interminable merry-go-round of an impersonal struggle for survival. They live in a world in which pressure for achievement is often unrelenting, in which business is business and politics is politics, in which love doesn't count and justice is a last resort. No wonder that under these conditions the man and the woman who meet in the privacy of the home as husband and wife or sit down at the table with their children as father and mother, are often beaten, tired, anxious individuals. They find great difficulty in creating in the few brief hours of conjugal privacy allotted to them the emotional atmosphere which will allow security and affection to flourish and to refresh them for the daily struggle. Thus within the family circle itself anxiety is often enhanced and the loss of meaning intensified and, desperately hurt, the human being continues his search for the meaning and community he has lost. At times, with the existentialist, he may indeed feel that all consensus is gone and only the anarchic uprooted individual remains to impose order by sheer force of will on the chaos which he inhabits.

It is in the search for community and meaning, including a sense of belonging and a new consensus on values, that the basic issues at the heart of our contemporary time of troubles are reflected. For the social change that ushered in the modern world destroyed both the ancient community and its world of values. In the world of accelerating flux and motion which succeeded the peasant village, no society has yet been able to offer on a permanent basis a new sense of community and an acceptable scheme of values. We have destroyed the old; few of us honestly desire its return. That which we called "the modern world" is changing irrevocably before our very eyes. We do not yet know the shape of things to come. This is the challenge of the ideological battle of the twentieth century. This is the heart of our concern with the responsibility of the church for the social order.

BIBLIOGRAPHY

Any reading list that attempts to cover the last several centuries of Western social history must necessarily be selective. The following books are intended primarily as suggestions to the reader who is interested in pursuing certain parts of the discussion in greater detail. On the changes in economic structure, both Kenneth Boulding, *The Organizational Revolution* (New York: Harper & Bros., 1953) and Peter Drucker, *The New Society* (New York: Harper & Bros., 1949) are informative. C. Wright Mills, *White Collar* (New York: Oxford University Press, 1951) traces changes in occupational and stratification patterns. Interesting materials on aspects of contemporary social change can be found in a series of readers issued by the Free Press, Glencoe, Ill.: cf. Paul Hatt and Albert J. Reiss, Jr. (eds.), *Reader in Urban Sociology* (1952); Robert K. Merton, *et al.*, *Reader in Bureaucracy* (1952); Morris Janowitz and Bernard Berelson (eds.), *Reader in Public Opinion and Communication* (1950); and Reinhard Bendix and Seymour Lipset, *Class, Status and Power* (1953). The same publisher is issuing the collected papers of Robert E. Park; both *Race and Culture* (1950) and *Human Communities* (1952) are full of highly perceptive and sensitive insights into the shape of modern society. Finally, David Riesman, *The Lonely Crowd* (New Haven: Yale Univ. Press, 1950) and Will Herberg, *Catholic–Protestant–Jew* (New York: Doubleday & Co., 1956) contain valuable accounts of the interrelations of institutions, ideas, and character.

CHAPTER 2

The Mind of Western Civilization

by Charles W. Kegley

What is meant by the "mind" of Western civilization? A helpful way to answer that question is to draw an analogy between a particular person and a designated civilization, for we know fairly well what we mean when we speak of the outlook or philosophy of life of a person. We ask these and similar questions: What are his basic assumptions? What belief or beliefs does he consciously and/or unconsciously use as the basis for his decisions, beliefs, actions, feelings, indeed his total conscious life? To interpret the "mind" of our civilization by analogy, we must try to identify and interpret the fundamental ideas not only of the intellectuals, scientists, philosophers, and the elite, but also to show how the ideas which control actual conduct arose and were put into practice as a way of living among the millions who carry the life stream of Western civilization. Because some of these ideas or beliefs are very abstract, our task is to interpret them clearly and to explain and illustrate the way in which these are expressed in the concrete actions and choices of the vast majority of people.

We study ideas and beliefs not only because they are the more important and enduring elements in human life, but equally because they are the sources of our actions. As Jesus probed the motives and beliefs of his contemporaries, or as a psychiatrist probes his patient today, so must we analyze the basic ideas and beliefs of people in order to understand them. All people, whether

Bushmen in Africa or members of the Institute for Advanced Studies at Princeton, do have controlling ideas and beliefs. The crucial questions are: What ideas actually dominate their thinking and so get expressed in action? Where did these ideas come from? What are their individual and social consequences? How may these results be evaluated? To examine the presuppositions of any civilization is a no less practical and urgent matter than for a surgeon to conduct a complete medical analysis before starting to operate.

Granting that contemporary Western culture is a complex, a milieu in which many important factors can be discerned, is there any basic theme or core of ideas which meaningfully interprets these complicated and ever-changing elements? The more one ponders the problem of understanding our culture today, the more one becomes convinced that underlying all the surface factors is a fundamental motif. The history of cultures, moreover, tends strongly to suggest that every major epoch reveals such a basic theme as its organizing and integrating factor. Thus, it is agreed that the basic motif of classical Greek life was philosophy, of Roman life, law, and of the Middle Ages—roughly, from Apostolic times to the sixteenth century—religion. What, now, is the fundamental motif of modern Western civilization? No one has perhaps better captured the answer to this question than Alfred North Whitehead, whose conclusions first appeared in his preface to *Science and the Modern World*. Whitehead writes:

. . . the mentality of an epoch springs from the view of the world which is, in fact, dominant in the educated sections of the communities in question. There may be more than one such scheme, corresponding to cultural divisions. The various human interests which suggest cosmologies, and also are influenced by them are science, aesthetics, ethics, and religion. In every age each of these topics suggests a view of the world. In so far as the same set of people are swayed by all, or more than one, of these interests, their effective outlook will be the joint production of these sources. But *each age has its dominant pre-occupation; and during the three centuries in question* [these past three] *the cosmology derived from science has been asserting itself at the expense of older points of view with their origins elsewhere.*[1]

We are prepared to assert that here, in essence, is an answer to the fundamental question posed in this part of our study. A basic motif of contemporary culture is science, and the main problems of our age derive from, in one way or another, and can best be understood in relation to, this "dominant preoccupation." Clearly, if evangelical Christianity is to address itself realistically to the issues of the culture in which it lives, it must know something of the forces which give rise to that motif. It must understand what modern science is and what it is not, and it must see in general how that basic motif has exhibited itself not only in the thought patterns, but equally in the ways of life of man today. After tracing the source and nature of the basic motif, we shall be better able to analyze more recent issues in Western thought and life at mid-century.

Although it is rarely a simple matter to describe how the dominant idea of an epoch came into being—whether the religious preoccupation of an earlier epoch, or the scientific preoccupation in our epoch—a brief account can be given of the rise and triumph of science in contemporary society. Its antecedents and roots, as well as its results and fruits, can be discerned. Those roots, generally speaking, are three in number.

ANTECEDENTS OF SCIENCE

If the sixteenth century stands out as a symbol of the beginnings of modern thought as these are exhibited in the religious realm, it is no less true that the same century witnessed the disruption of the old order and the rise of modern science. Again, to repeat the parallel, if Reformation Day, October 31, 1517—

[1] New York: Macmillan Co., 1927, p. ix. Italics mine.

43

the day on which Luther posted the Ninety-five Theses on the church door at Wittenberg—symbolizes the beginning of modern religious thought and life, then the year 1600, the year in which Giordano Bruno, a defender of freedom of thought, was martyred in Rome, may be taken as a symbol of the ushering in of modern science in the strict sense of the term. The first, and perhaps the most important mark of the beginning of modern science, is expressed in Bruno, and in Francis Bacon's *Advancement of Learning* which appeared in 1605. This was the emphasis upon the technique of observation.

It is almost impossible to exaggerate the importance of the difference between the ways in which it was assumed that we come to the truth before this symbolic year and the ways in which, ever since, it is taken for granted by modern inquirers that we arrive at truths. Prior to the sixteenth century, with certain remarkable exceptions, it had been assumed that truth came either by processes of pure thought, such as the deduction of specific truths from general axioms, or by revelation, or by consulting ancient or contemporary "authorities" such as Aristotle or Roman Catholic church dogma. From the year 1600, which we use as a symbol, it has increasingly been assumed that we arrive at truth in any sphere, and concerning any problem, by using what is now the first step in scientific thinking, namely, observation. There is a story which in spite of its exaggeration, and its familiarity in some circles, nonetheless aptly illustrates this first main point. It is alleged that a group of monks in a thirteenth-century monastery were discussing far into the night, and with excitement which matched their great learning, the question of how many teeth there are in a horse's mouth. Starting with what they took to be the axioms that God is good, and that he is the creator of all that exists, they tried to reason with impressive skill how many teeth there accordingly must be in the horse's mouth. Unhappily, they could come to no agreement. As hour after hour passed, so the story runs, the village nitwit, who was outside taking care of the carriages, and who had by this time been informed by the servants of the profound problem being discussed, finally burst into the room exclaiming, "Couldn't one of you reverend gentlemen come out and open the horse's mouth here and count the teeth?"

In a more sophisticated way, William James almost 200 years later emphasized this same insistence upon observation. When he was finishing his famous *Principles of Psychology*, William James wrote in a letter to his brother, Henry, "I have to forge every sentence in the teeth of irreducible and stubborn fact." If space permitted, one could illustrate this movement away from the use of the deductive method and of authority with countless examples chosen from physics, astronomy, biology, and related fields; but the field of psychology serves dramatically to illustrate the point. The titles of books and courses of study, for example, express the complete difference in approach between the older and the modern methods of study in psychology. Prior to the appearance of scientific method, the study of human nature generally went under the name of "rational" or "soul" psychology, consisting of impressive and speculative efforts at introspection and the examination of the psyche or soul of man as a spiritual being. The studies were as verbose as they were useless. Progress was made for the first time when empirical psychology, in the hands of Wundt and James, used the techniques of observation and described as precisely as possible the nature of the psychophysical organism that we call man.

This insistent interest in irreducible and stubborn facts constitutes one of the characteristics of present-day efforts to arrive at understanding. It would be interesting to trace the history of this persistent emphasis upon observation in all the important areas of study which have grown up since the sixteenth century. In the same spring of 1616 in which Shakespeare and Cervantes died, Harvey is believed to have first expounded his theory of the circulation of the blood. In the year that Galileo died (1642),

Newton was born. And from Galileo—who may safely be called one of the first great modern scientists—there was passed on to Newton the intellectual passion for precise observation which is the keynote of all modern scientific procedure. Within this magnificent period, which almost outshines the brilliant Periclean age in Greece, there lived and worked such men as Bacon, Harvey, Galileo, Descartes, Pascal, Leeuwenhoek, Huygens, Boyle, Newton, Locke, Spinoza, and Leibniz—to list only the sacred number of twelve. Central in the work of all of these men, and in the efforts of others from many different fields, is the emphasis upon the absolute necessity of accurate observation and classification of phenomena to arrive at an understanding of man and of the universe in which he lives.

Another factor in the rise of modern science is the development of mathematics. This may at first strike one as strange. Did not mathematics appear as a significant feature of the thinking of ancient Greek civilization? Indeed, did not Pythagoras, over six centuries before Jesus, make mathematics central to his entire philosophy? How, then, dare it be asserted that in the rise of mathematics, we witness one of the main factors in the development of the modern *Weltanschauung* (world view)? The answer is that mathematics, as with the general spirit of the inquiring mind, has undergone fundamental changes within the past 300 years, and these changes and developments have helped to produce, even as they went hand-in-hand with, the growth of modern science. It has been asserted by Bertrand Russell and his associates that the science of pure mathematics, in its modern developments, may claim to be one of the more original creations of the human mind. There are two features of the modern science of pure mathematics which, taken together, spell out its tremendous significance in the making of the modern mind.

For one thing, in the past few centuries mathematics has developed further than ever before into a pure science. In primitive and prescientific cultures, peoples tended to think of number only as it applied to or was exhibited in certain objects. Thus, men normally had ten fingers and ten toes; here are seven chairs, there are twelve people. But an immense step in the human capacity for abstraction was taken when men began to construct, not only simple mathematical tables, but geometric and algebraic systems, the symbols of which were entirely abstracted from any particular entities. Relationships were consciously developed between groups of symbols—number, shapes such as squares, circles, and the like—and finally symbols which themselves stood for mathematical operations. Thus Whitehead can write that modern pure mathematics is "thought moving in the sphere of complete abstraction from any particular instance of what it is talking about." [2]

A second feature of mathematics as an antecedent of modern science is the remarkable accident (though in a sense, of course, it was no accident) that the inventive minds that constructed modern mathematical systems were the same minds that saw its significance when applied to the sciences and to philosophy generally. History would certainly have been different if the French philosopher Descartes had not discovered analytical geometry, and Newton and Leibniz had not invented infinitesimal calculus. The everyday world in which the reader of these words lives is in large measure what it is because these magnificent minds who fathered the modern scientific world thought that their mathematical theories reflected the "laws of nature" and could be used, therefore, in interpreting natural phenomena. Indeed, mathematics formed one of the indispensable intellectual instruments with which all men of science approach the observation of nature. Galileo, Descartes, Huygens, Newton, Leibniz—and from these men to Einstein—all contributed to the science of pure mathematics at the same time they developed modern science. Without this amazing development of mathematics in

[2] Whitehead, *op. cit.*, p. 32.

these four centuries, most if not all of the present-day scientific development would have been impossible.

A third main antecedent condition which prepared the way for the birth and growth of science in the modern world was the so-called instinctive belief in the detailed and universal order of nature. This idea should be sufficiently clear to every high school graduate today to spare us the task of explaining and documenting the belief. To get the best understanding of the belief in the universal order of nature, we should try to place ourselves in the world of thought prior to the modern era and to see imaginatively what one's outlook would be like if this assumption of orderliness were not made. Imagine what our attitude toward the universe and our fellowmen would be if we simply took it for granted that both nature and human nature were under the control of, or were the media for the expression of, spiritual beings of one sort or another, that is, angels, gods, demons, and the like. Little wonder, if one makes such assumptions, that miracles should be expected to occur at any time and place, that witchcraft should be accepted by presumably educated people, and that the end of the world should be expected at any time. More important still, little wonder that to only a very few minds it should occur that all events—those in the psychical and spiritual as well as every event in the "natural" world—should be subject to some universal principles of growth and development.

Yet it was precisely this idea of the universal and detailed order of the universe which arose with modern science and which helped in turn to create the soil in which science could grow. Once a Copernicus could create the revolution in thought that the sun and not the earth is the center of all that exists in the universe, and a Darwin could suggest that in all levels of life, from the lowest to the highest, a principle of evolution from the lower to the higher was at work—once these and other hypotheses could be set forth on the basis of the uniformity of nature—then it was simply a matter of time until a clergyman by the name of Henry Drummond could write a book entitled *The Natural Law in the Spiritual World*.

SCIENCE, SCIENTIFIC METHOD, "SCIENTISM," AND THEIR SIGNIFICANCE FOR CONTEMPORARY CULTURE

If we now have an understanding of some of the factors which preceded and preconditioned modern science, we may ask precisely what we mean today by "science," "scientific method," and "scientism." These three terms need to be distinguished carefully, and we need to see their proper meaning as expressed in the culture of the Western world today.

First of all, however, it is imperative to disabuse our minds of a view of science which has been widely held and which, because it is largely erroneous, must be identified and rejected before we can address our attention to an analysis of contemporary problems. Originally, the term science, which comes from the Latin word *scire*, to know, referred to any disciplined, organized body of knowledge. So understood, one might speak of almost any field of study—from tent making to theology—as a science, meaning by that the orderly statement of what is known or believed at any given time by a group of people. A certain textbook in theology which appeared at the beginning of the twentieth century, for instance, asked in its first chapter whether theology was a science, and proceeded to answer that of course it was because it consisted of a systematic body of knowledge.[3] Obviously, this definition of science is completely unacceptable today because it simply is not what is meant by the term when used by its exponents in, for example, the physical, biological, and social sciences.

When we ask what the term science does mean when properly used, we come upon one of the rock-bottom issues in contem-

[3] H. E. Jacobs, *A Summary of The Christian Faith* (Philadelphia: United Lutheran Publication House, 1905), p. 1.

porary thought and life. The term "science" has come to stand in our age for a method, for a way of arriving at truth in any sphere whatever. It is the contemporary answer to the question, "How do we know?"

Before we can ask what significance the emphasis upon scientific method may have, we must first ask, "What is this method?"

First, all users of the scientific method bring to their inquiry, as we have already seen, an almost religious passion for the objective observation and classification of all facts. The attitude of science has long been described as disinterestedness. This is nowhere better expressed than in Huxley's famous exhortation to "sit down before the facts as a little child, and let them lead you where they will." Whether it be the question, "Is the earth flat?" or the question, "Is man a sinner?," the scientific frame of mind demands first of all the absolutely objective observing of all the facts relevant to the question, regardless of the conclusion to which these seem to point.

The second step which follows the observation and classification of the facts is the imaginative creation of an "hypothesis." The word hypothesis comes from the Greek *hypo* (under) and *titheni* (to place), suggesting that when the hypothesis is placed under the actual evidence as a foundation it will support that evidence. In other words, it is a tentative and provisional thesis or proposed explanation on the basis of which one may draw conclusions. Scientists and logicians customarily speak of certain criteria of a good hypothesis. These are usually four in number: (1) that it be capable of being proved or disproved by the facts; (2) that it allows one to make predictions about expected events; (3) that it be consistent with all other facts and hypotheses; and finally, (4) that it be the simplest possible accounting for the facts.

When the supporting evidence has been gathered and the best hypothesis has been tested and thus confirmed or verified, the scientist speaks of his tentative explanation as a theory. It should be noted that the theory, and that which we shall shortly describe as the conclusion, are set forth with the greatest care and hesitation and always in a tentative fashion. A classic illustration of the first and second steps is found in Darwin's record of his careful gathering of material over a period of many years before he could reorganize it into a meaningful whole.

In October, 1838, that is fifteen months after I had begun my systematic inquiry, I happened to read for amusement, Malthus on *Population,* and being well prepared to appreciate the struggle for existence which everywhere goes on, from long-continued observations of the habits of animals and plants, it at once struck me that under these circumstances favorable variations would tend to be preserved, and unfavorable ones destroyed. The result of this would be the formation of new species. *Here then I had at last got a theory by which to work,* but I was so anxious to avoid prejudice that I determined not for some time to write even the briefest sketch of it. In June, 1842, I first allowed myself the satisfaction of writing a brief abstract of my theory in pencil, in thirty-five pages, and this was enlarged during the summer of 1844, into one of 230 pages.[4]

The final step in scientific method is, of course, the drawing of a conclusion on the basis of hypothesis which has been repeatedly confirmed.[5]

It should be noted here that the methods of confirmation vary with the nature of the field in which the hypothesis is made. For example, if in the exact physical sciences the question is, "What is the boiling point of water?," it is possible for even the amateur experimenter to confirm at any time under controlled laboratory conditions the conclusion that water boils at 212°F. at sea level. In less exact fields such as the social and historical sciences, however, the evidence which confirms hypotheses must be sought among quite diverse events, facts, and circumstances, and under

[4] Quoted in H. L. Searles, *Logic and Scientific Method* (New York: Ronald Press Co., 1948), p. 161.

[5] We prefer to speak of confirmation rather than verification because the latter word literally means "to make true" or "to prove true," whereas the word confirmation refers to the continual successful testing of a hypothesis.

conditions which can by no means always be controlled. Clearly, as one moves from the physical to the biological, to the social, and finally to the religious field, for example, the scientific method is used with less and less precision and confidence.

"Scientism" has become a popular word, defined as an increasing tendency on the part of different writers in several fields to limit science and scientific method in two ways: to claim that scientific method is the only valid and fruitful way of knowing; and further to restrict this method so that nothing is admitted to have "meaning" unless it can be confirmed via sense data. It is our belief that both of these limitations are unwarranted and, indeed, dangerous. Moreover, as Hocking well expresses it, ". . . science has not yet accepted this voice as its own." [6] It should be said as clearly as possible that thus to find fault with "scientism" is emphatically not equivalent to condemning other interpretations of scientific method and of the nature of confirmation in the use of that method. To draw an analogy: Rejection of homeopathic medical practitioners in the medical profession is certainly not the same as the rejection of the whole medical profession. A bit of clarification of each of the above elements of what we call "scientism" is needed. We shall consider the latter element first.

What is involved here is the temper or attitude voiced for almost a quarter of a century and now known as the voice of logical positivism. The logical positivists—who, incidentally, would gladly run for the office of official spokesmen for all true science —begin with a laudable concern for precise methods of thinking. They quickly inform us, however, that the task of logic and of philosophy is to develop a critically exact terminology and a logic without ontology. The only statements which have meaning are those which are subject to confirmation in terms of observable sense data. Any propositions which have to do with the realm of values or metaphysics are accordingly ruled out by

[6] W. E. Hocking, *Science and The Idea of God* (Chapel Hill: Univ. of North Carolina Press, 1944), p. 6.

definition—that is, by the definition of "meaning." Totality statements and value judgments are thereby denounced as meaningless. Judgments about "the real" as distinct from phenomenal space-time objects, or about good and evil, beauty and ugliness, and the like, can make no claim to truth or falsity. They may be uttered as mere opinion, taste, or feeling, but they cannot possibly claim to be statements based on knowledge. Why not? Because they have no meaning in the sense that their presumed truth or falsity can be confirmed via observable sensory experience.

In this brief sketch of scientific method and scientism, we cannot enter into a lengthy evaluation of such a movement as logical positivism, but it is relevant to our study to point out that contemporary positivism is, in the minds of many scientists and philosophers, a misreading of the nature of scientific method. To allow it to claim the right to speak for scientific method is to invite trouble both for the full and legitimate use of scientific method on the one hand, and for its applications to special fields of study on the other hand.[7]

The other aspect of scientism is likewise of utmost importance for our understanding of contemporary culture, especially in religious thought and life. The point to be grasped is this: Modern man is increasingly being converted to the belief that there is one and only one way to knowledge: scientific method. John Dewey, whose claim to fame is scarcely based on his clarity, probably has stated at least this issue more clearly and emphatically than anyone else when he writes that the use of scientific method is the mark of the modern truth seeker regardless of the field in which he works. Thus, for example, whether the problem we are trying to solve arises in physics, biology, sociology, or theology, the answer to the question is to be found by modern

[7] See Richard von Mises, *Positivism: A Study in Human Understanding* (Cambridge: Harvard Univ. Press, 1951) for an excellent recent work both of explanation and of criticism of this school of thought in the sciences and philosophy.

man not by reading a Bible, by consulting a religious authority, or sitting and pondering it by pure reason, but by the experimental inquiry of the scientific method. Our conclusion, moreover, whether it be about the flatness of the earth or the nature of God, cannot possibly be more than tentative and probable. It is not too strong to say that the student of contemporary problems who does not understand this essential mark of the modern mentality can scarcely deal adequately with major individual and collective problems today.

In his Terry Lectures at Yale University, 1936, Professor Dewey wrote a statement which has become classic. Because it set forth so succinctly and forcefully the issues that are involved, we quote four paragraphs.

It is no part of my intention to rehearse in any detail the weighty facts that collectively go by the name of the conflict of science and religion—a conflict that is not done away with by calling it a conflict of science with theology, as long as even a minimum of intellectual assent is prescribed as essential. The impact of astronomy not merely upon the older cosmogony of religion but upon elements of creeds dealing with historic events—witness the idea of ascent into heaven—is familiar. Geological discoveries have displaced creation myths which once bulked large. Biology has revolutionized conceptions of soul and mind which once occupied a central place in religious beliefs and ideas, and this science has made a profound impression upon ideas of sin, redemption, and immortality. Anthropology, history and literary criticism have furnished a radically different version of the historic events and personages upon which Christian religions have built. Psychology is already opening to us natural explanations of phenomena so extraordinary that once their supernatural origin was, so to say, the natural explanation.

The significant bearing for my purpose of all this is that new methods of inquiry and reflection have become for the educated man today the final arbiter of all questions of fact, existence, and intellectual assent. Nothing less than a revolution, in the "seat of intellectual authority," has taken place. This revolution, rather than any particular aspect of its impact upon this and that religious belief, is the central thing. In this revolution, every defeat is a stimulus to renewed inquiry, every victory won is the open door to more discoveries, and every discovery is a new seed planted in the soil of intelligence, from which grow fresh plants with new fruits. The mind of man is being habituated to a new method and ideal: there is but one sure road of access to truth—the road of patient, cooperative inquiry operating by means of observation, experiment, record and controlled reflection.

The scope of the change is well illustrated by the fact that whenever a particular outpost is surrendered it is usually met by the remark from a liberal theologian that the particular doctrine or supposed historic or literary tenet surrendered was never, after all, an intrinsic part of religious belief, and that without it the true nature of religion stands out more clearly than before. Equally significant is the growing gulf between fundamentalists and liberals in the churches. What is not realized—although perhaps it is more definitely seen by fundamentalists than by liberals—is that the issue does not concern this and that piecemeal item of belief, but centers in the question of the method by which any and every item of intellectual belief is to be arrived at and justified.

The positive lesson is that religious qualities and values if they are real at all are not bound up with any single item of intellectual assent, not even that of the existence of the God of theism; and that, under existing conditions, the religious function in experience can be emancipated only through surrender of the whole notion of special truths that are religious by their own nature, together with the idea of peculiar avenues of access to such truths. For were we to admit that there is but one method for ascertaining fact and truth—that conveyed by the word "scientific" in its most general and generous sense—no discovery in any branch of knowledge and inquiry could then disturb the faith that is religious. I should describe this faith as the unification of the self through allegiance to inclusive ideal ends, which imagination presents to us and to which the human will responds as worthy of controlling our desires and choices.[8]

INFLUENCE OF SCIENTIFIC OUTLOOK UPON LIFE OF ORDINARY MAN

In order better to understand the practical significance of this scientific mentality, we should ask, "How has it altered the day-

[8] John Dewey, *A Common Faith* (New Haven: Yale Univ. Press, 1934), pp. 31-33.

to-day attitudes and habits of the man of the street?" Recognizing that volumes could be written in answer to the question, we suggest the following main evidences of its influences:

1. Modern science has enormously enlarged the amount of the universe open to the mind of the plain man. Contrast, for example, the world picture of Martin Luther as a university student with that of a university student today. For Luther, the Ptolemaic view was taken for granted. According to this theory the earth is the center of everything and man, of course, is the central creature of the earth. Moreover, the flat earth was believed to have come into existence in about 4004 B.C., and consisted of what we now call central Europe, the Near East, and some vague section known as the Orient. No wonder it seemed natural to assume that God was intimately concerned with the actions of all his little children. But today every college student knows that the Copernican revolution correctly describes the sun as the center of the solar system. Our planet appears as a minor satellite of one of the smaller stars which in turn is one infinitesimal part of an immeasurable system. An instructor in physics, for example, might readily quote Sir Arthur Eddington's estimate that there are fifteen figenquintillion atoms in this space-time universe. Why then should not our modern young friend feel a great gulf between whatever power controls "this mysterious universe" and his own puny life and petty concerns?

2. The modern mentality is influenced through the constant maxim of scientific interpretation, namely, universal law. It is one of the presuppositions of the exact sciences that this is a law-abiding universe. Were it not, how could we predict anything with reference to the activities of man's body or the movements of the planets? The supreme goal of science, it may be said, is the unification of knowledge within a single all-embracing system. Einstein in his last years believed he was on the verge of discovering the uniform interpretation of all reality through a single

all-sufficient principle, one which would combine the general theory of relativity and the principle of gravitation.

3. Modern man, moreover, knows the tendency of science to interpret everything as a process, a becoming. In a sense this is the recognition of the process of evolution written into the entire universe, which means that it holds for most modern men not only of the physical and biological spheres, but of the social and ethical as well. There is not a field, including theology, which is unaffected by this emphasis.

4. Probably the greatest practical impact of science upon modern man is in the development of a scientific civilization. I can think of no more compelling symbol of this fact than the way in which the towers of old Trinity Church in Manhattan—towers which for the previous epoch symbolized the dominance of religion—are now dwarfed and darkened by the towering steel and concrete of a mechanized civilization. The church, which was reared to the glory of God, strains to fill its pews for an hour or two on Sunday, whereas the skyscrapers, reared to the glory of man and his ingenuity, are overcrowded five days of the week with the throbbing, even if often neurotic, life of the twentieth century.

This effect of science upon the day-to-day life of modern man is pointedly described in the following poem:

The March of Science

First, dentistry was painless;
Then bicycles were chainless
And carriages were horseless
And many laws, enforceless.

Next, cookery was fireless,
Telegraphy was wireless,
Cigars were nicotineless
And coffee, caffeinless.

Soon oranges were seedless,
The putting green was weedless,
The college boy was hatless,
The proper diet, fatless.

Now motor roads are dustless,
The latest steel is rustless,
Our tennis courts are sodless,
Our new religions, godless.[9]

Before we ask how this basic motif of science finds its expression in contemporary life, two observations should be made.

The first is that the scientific method has the characteristic of universality, and thus commends itself as competent to be the integrating factor of this epoch. In this respect it may be compared to philosophy in the Greek epoch, or religion from the fifth to the sixteenth centuries. Each of these fundamental preoccupations served to integrate the thinking and life of a culture. Science likewise claims to have this same capacity. In the preceding epoch, it has frequently been observed, the *commune vinculuum* or common bond of all literate peoples in the Western world was their training in the traditional subjects of the medieval university and their common outlook upon the world expressed in the Catholic faith. But the common bond of Western society today certainly has a different basis, and this basis is none other than the scientific method which all peoples everywhere can use and which forms, therefore, the bridge between otherwise conflicting nations and cultures. As Radhakrishnan writes: "There are no competing scientific cultures as there are competing religions or competing codes of law." [10] Man and his universe, it is claimed, can be understood and controlled by using the scientific method.

[9] Arthur Guiterman, from *Gaily The Troubadour* (New York: E. P. Dutton & Co., Inc., 1936).

[10] *The Philosophy of Sarvepalli Radhakrishnan*, ed. Paul A. Schilpp (New York: Tudor Publishing Co., 1952), p. 17.

It is by this means that man's health and happiness can be cultivated, and the method is the same regardless of race, color, or creed. Any problem man faces, from cancer research to the nature and use of the atom bomb, is a problem to be solved by use of this universally-accepted method.

A second observation concerns the generally unrealized rate of speed with which modern science has developed. Note that it is not merely the speed to which we point, but the rate at which that development has taken place. A single illustration will serve our purpose. Consider the progress of scientific knowledge from the year 1560, immediately before the births of Galileo and Kepler, to the year 1700, when Newton was at the height of his fame. This is a mere one hundred and forty years, and represents the infancy of science. Nonetheless, in that brief span greater progress was made in the scientific understanding of man and his universe than was achieved in the Greek, Roman, Egyptian, Indian, and Chinese cultures of the ancient period, which was ten times as long. The rate of development and application of science has of course again greatly increased in the twentieth century. As Sir James Jeans writes:

The last hundred years have seen more change than a thousand years of the Roman Empire, more than a hundred thousand years of the Stone Age. This change has resulted in large part from the applications of physical science, electricity and petrol, and by way of the various industrial arts, now affects almost every moment of our existences. Its use in medicine and surgery may save our lives; its use in warfare may involve us in utter ruination. In its more abstract aspects it has exerted a powerful influence on our philosophies, our religions and our general outlook of life.[11]

If anyone asks, "What has all this got to do with the many practical personal and social issues today—with unemployment, birth control, race relations, and the like?," the answer is: "Every-

[11] *The Growth of Physical Science* (New York: Macmillan Co., 1947), p. 1.

thing." For these issues, and others which with them flood upon us, receive their present-day expression because of the basic thought-pattern of science and its technological pattern which undergirds modern life. In any distraught epoch, it can be said that unless one patiently probes into the deeper, less easily discernible forces which are at work, one fails completely either properly to diagnose or wisely prescribe for its ills. Any failure to understand the basic mentality of our age makes it certain that we shall not effect a cure, but merely treat symptoms. What we need, if a homely analogy may be used, is not a salve or ointment for this boil and that carbuncle, but a metabolism test and blood analysis which will reveal the underlying causes of the trouble.

OTHER "SIGNS OF THE TIMES"

Every perceptive critic of our age discerns the contradictions and dilemmas in our thought and life. In addition to modern man's preoccupation with science and the scientific method, and often connected with it, there are certain tensions in the thinking of our culture which must be examined if a clear picture is to be drawn of the main characteristics of present-day attitudes. These tensions are in the area of religious attitudes, in our obsession with "things," in intellectualism vs. anti-intellectualism, in individualism vs. collectivism, and in war vs. international law.

RELIGION IGNORED AND RELIGION "ENJOYED"

In the area of religious attitudes, a whole group of trends has served to crystallize the deep-seated dilemma of materialistic secularism vs. religion "enjoyed." We must examine both poles of this tension, and see them *in* tension if we are not to oversimplify and misread the mind of our time.

John Bennett's description has become classic; he said secularism "is life organized apart from God." [12] It is the total way

[12] John C. Bennett, *Christianity and Our World* (New York: The Edward W. Hazen Foundation, 1936), p. 1. See also the illuminating study by

of thinking and habit of life which simply disregards God and religious values. It is not that most modern men, as some critics erroneously suppose, passionately argue against the existence of God and the organized expresssion of religion in life; it is rather that they ignore this point of view. It is to them largely irrelevant. Man is so completely convinced of the competence of science to bring him health and happiness, to relieve his drudgery and solve his problems, that he simply has lost interest in Irresistible Grace.

Contrast the central preoccupation of the secularist with that of the preceding epoch. The citizen of the middle ages literally considered heaven to be his home. He was a mere traveler in this temporary earthly life—"a sojourner among strangers in a strange land." Man's supreme goal was to achieve eternal salvation. Who, now, could for a moment seriously maintain that this is the consuming interest of the average citizen of the Western world today? The chances are that your next door neighbors and mine are overwhelmingly concerned with their life in *this* world. In place of the catechetical statements quoted above, some of the axioms by which most modern men live have frequently been expressed as follows:

1. The main object in life is to enjoy it to the full here and now.
2. Nobody knows what is beyond death, therefore, it is only common sense to increase the goods and enrich the experiences of this world. "Enjoy yourself, it's later than you think." "You can't take it with you."
3. There is no absolute truth, no absolute beauty, no absolute goodness. All things are relative.
4. To be wise and human is to be tolerant. And this means that not to admit the same degree of truth to an opponent's position as you claim for your own is to be bigoted and intolerant.

Georgia Harkness, *Secularism, the Modern Rival of Christian Faith* (New York: Abingdon-Cokesbury, 1952) and the much needed warning of Edward A. Aubrey against using "secularism" to stand for anything we're against in *Secularism as a Myth* (New York: Harper & Bros., 1954).

5. Justice is equality, hence, any kind of inequality, of income, social security, or political right is unjust. Economic, political and social rights means the same general income, authority, and standing for everybody.
6. Religion, like art, or music, is the nice activity and expression of human nature. Anyone who wishes to may practice it providing he minds his own business in so doing.

Finally, this attitude of indifference to religion may be seen in any one of the major spheres of contemporary life. Consider education, music, and art.

For example, the Greek and premodern epochs exalted in educational theory and in practice the knowledge of goodness, truth, and beauty. It was claimed in these eras that the highest knowledge was knowledge of God. Theology was the queen of the "sciences." The saint and the scholar were, in ideal at least, embodied in the same man, from Augustine to Luther. The central affirmations of the Christian creeds constituted the core and organizing center of all learning, so that ultimate wisdom was in understanding the truth "once for all delivered to the saints." Of course, something of this philosophy of education was, and still is, embodied in the Western world of the past three hundred years. But today the full impact of secularism, child of the scientific mentality, has been felt in all levels of the educational system from grammar through graduate schools. A case might easily be made that secularism's influence in the latter type of school has become increasingly significant during the past quarter of a century, for the graduates of these schools have become the administrators and teachers of the lower levels in the educational system.[13] The fact that much of the severest criticism of secularism in education which is voiced at present by teachers and administrators of institutions of higher learning in America reinforces rather than contradicts this point.

[13] An excellent aid in the study of the mutual problems of education and religion today is: Amos Wilder (ed.), *Liberal Learning and Religion* (New York: Harper & Bros., 1951).

Now the effect of this *Weltanschauung* is clearly evidenced (and its relations to science clearly seen) in at least four respects. First, it is seen in the view that education has no permanent and enduring object or goal. Its purposes and aims change with the change of the cultural setting. Secondly, emphasis is placed on teaching students how to think, not what to think. The modern educator knows no more deadly sin than indoctrination. To inflame the intellect and unsettle the adolescent beliefs of students was the description given by a former American university president— one who, ironically, was at the same time accused by his more "scientific" colleagues of being an obscurantist and flirter with medievalism! Thirdly, secularism has worked as an acid in the educational system to remove almost all trace of the nature and role of religion in life. Not only is religion itself largely eliminated from the American public school system, including state and many private universities, but all other subjects, including history and literature, for example, are taught generally in such a way, and with such emphasis, that the American youth would never imagine from what he learns in school that religion is or was a significant factor in American life. It is no exaggeration to say that American life is thus described in substance as godless.

Finally, the emphasis of most American education falls more and more upon self-expression—as in progressive education— and upon so-called education for citizenship, or for a particular profession, trade, or technical skill. This emphatically has one psychological effect upon the student: to cultivate in him the conviction that the dominant, if not exclusive, purpose of his education is to prepare for the job which will pay him the most money and, he may hope, incidentally, be best fitted to his skills. Obviously, to speak to such a person about his "vocation" is to induce a blank stare. Of the almost innumerable instances which could be cited to document this assertion, one of the clearer is contained in the now famous special study by *Time* magazine on

"The Younger Generation" which, incidentally, the editors shrewdly call the "silent generation." A single paragraph follows:

On a sunny Sunday not long ago, Sociology Professor Carr B. Lavell of George Washington University took one of his students on a fishing trip. He is a brilliant student, president of his class, a big man on campus, evidently with a bright future in his chosen field, medicine. In the bracing air, professor and student had a quiet talk. Why had he gone into medicine? asked the professor. Answer: medicine looked lucrative. What did he want to do as a doctor? Get into the specialty that offered biggest fees. Did he think that a doctor owed some special service to the community? Probably not. "I am just like anyone else," said the student. "I just want to prepare myself so that I can get the most out of it for me. I hope to make a lot of money in a hurry. I'd like to retire in about ten years and do the things I really want to do." And what are those? "Oh," said the brilliant student, "fishing, traveling, taking it easy."

Then they stopped talking, because the student had a nibble.[14]

Education which once had goodness, truth, and beauty as its center and goal now has as its holy method a sacred science which scarcely is scientific.

Secularism, as religious values ignored, can also be seen in the music and art of our age. A single set of contrasts in each field will serve our purpose. The music of Bach or Beethoven, for example, was dominantly preoccupied with the basic themes of life and death, hope and fear, love and hate. The meanings which such music conveyed were philosophical and religious, and the framework in which their fundamental contributions were made was that of good and evil, in short, the basic issues of life. Contrast their symphonies and chorals with a contemporary American symphony whose title is *Impressions of a Perambulator Going Down Fifth Avenue*, or with Ferde Grofé's widely hailed *Grand Canyon Suite*, the most popular section of which describes the hee hawing of a jackass. Music, it has been said, expresses the

[14] *Time* (November 5, 1951).

deepest life of the spirit of man and of his culture. If this is so, then the soul of modern man is apparently either an empty void or has in it little more to express than violent syncopation and impressionistic reactions to a depersonalized and meaningless world.

Nor is the situation very different in the field of art. We are familiar generally with the works of art of the past epochs, and their themes and scope clearly indicate the basic preoccupation of their minds: witness Michelangelo. By contrast, one gets the full force of the scientific and secular spirit in much of the impressionism and expressionism of the contemporary galleries. In public lectures recently delivered at Columbia University, Lewis Mumford gave exceptionally clear expression to this point. He wrote:

In those special realms of art, above all painting, that once recorded the greatest freedom and creativeness, we find in our age that the symbols of deepest expression of emotion and feeling are a succession of dehumanized nightmares. . . . At times (today) the emotion is so lacerating that the next step beyond would be either insanity or suicide, violence and nihilism; the death of human personality. This is the message that modern art brings to us at its purest.

The maimed fantasies, the organized frustrations that we see in every comprehensive exhibition of painting today are the evidence of a deeper personal abdication. Pattern and purpose have all but disappeared, along with the person who once, in his own right, embodied them. Man has become an exile in this mechanical world, or even worse, he has become a displaced person.[15]

The minds of the prize-winning artists appear to be either blank or perverted. Certainly not nature or the great creative experiences of life inspire such grotesque, distorted, and meaningless shapes and colors, but rather a mentality afflicted with a "sickness unto death."

[15] Public lectures at Columbia by Lewis Mumford, quoted in *Time*, (May 7, 1951), p. 67.

If earlier epochs produced art which was symphonic in its proportions, secularism appears chiefly to produce that which is convulsive or trivial in character.[16] But the portrait of secularism in modern art would not be accurate if it did not also take cognizance of the serious attempts of many artists, as in architecture, to make the most of a completely this-worldly philosophy of life. Even the science of photography, for example (so symbolic of a mechanized civilization!), strives valiantly to become, and often succeeds in becoming, an art. Perhaps even here, though, it becomes an inspiration precisely because it captures the sudden burst of laughter of a child, or the surging power of a ship in the high sea. Again, architecture, which gleefully ridicules Gothic "nightmares," achieves the soundness and simplicity so appealing in genuinely functional structures. Where its beauty does appear, it is in the service of utility. And this is the lesson we have been learning: that secularism, the child of science, controls the this-worldly, self-centered, spirit of our age.

This ignoring of religion dramatizes all the more the dilemma, for our age is also characterized by a "return to religion," to an exaltation of it in areas and ways which are astonishing. Turn on the radio or juke box and witness the oddest example of religiosity, the lovers behind every chapel and chiming bell that Tin Pan Alley can imagine. Or hear a British visitor's description:

I was recently in a bar presided over by a former star of the Howard Athenaeum (of Boston). It was full of young people "horsing around," as the saying goes. A young man and young woman were wrapt in the pursuit of love and were feeding nickels, more or less automatically, into the juke-box. They gazed into each other's eyes to the tune of "Steam Heat" (the title tells all). Then came "The

[16] That journal of amazing discernment of our time, *The New Yorker*, has twice in recent years commented with caustic effectiveness on this point via cartoons. One showed two women, one of whom having sat before a particularly wild but prize-winning instance of impressionism, finally says, "But dearie, it must mean something."

Man Upstairs," but as I left the bar *Eros* was winning over *Agape* hands down." [17]

If we listen to the music, to the loudest congressmen, or ponder those edifying statistics, or learn how "We Can Be Happy" in Sunday morning's sermon and how "We Need Not Be Unhappy" in Sunday evening's sermon—who can deny that America is discovering religion? Or is it such a dangerous substitute that we wouldn't know the gospel if we heard it?

HEDONISM—WITH MISGIVINGS

Finally, the basic core of our culture is seen in persistent preoccupation—one might as well have said obsession—with things, with the material as being the most real and important.[18] One hesitates to use the phrase "materialistic hedonism" because it points to certain ways of thinking and living regnant in the past. But thanks to technology and its fruits—a technicology which is the important product of modern science—this is perhaps as good a way as any to describe this aspect of our culture.

For any widely adopted philosophy of life, there is usually a good reason to be found. The modern, sophisticated, materialistic hedonism, which began in the eighteenth century but has only now come to full growth, is a reaction to several major factors. For one thing, it is folly to close our eyes to the immense contribution which the physical, biological, and social sciences have made to the life of the common man. To science must go the credit for discovering the cure for many formerly deadly diseases, for producing enough food, clothing, and shelter for all the peoples of the earth if our resources were co-operatively used, for relieving the common man and woman of much of their

[17] D. W. Brogan, "God and the Juke-Box," *Manchester Guardian*, Oct. 14, 1954.

[18] Far from irrelevant is the comment of a Korean War veteran who, discharged from the army, re-enlisted at once at 17 years of age, explaining, "I'm going to stay in the army. Where else can I retire when I'm 37?" Quoted in *Quick* (February 25, 1952), p. 25.

drudgery and labor, and for giving the light, power, and countless devices which make everyday tasks easier. If the Industrial Revolution and capitalism brought problems, they also make the entire earthly environment of Joe Smith, the average American citizen of today, a vastly more livable one than his great-grandfather had. All this is important, but it is also so familiar as to require no review here. The one point that it is imperative to see is that our friend Joe has come to believe that science can do anything that needs to be done to make him healthy, wealthy, and happy. It is no accident that the slogan of a major chemical company weekly sang its philosophy, like a sermon of old, into his radio, "Better things for better living . . ." Through religion? Through philosophy? Oh no, through science!

The two aspects of this point of view which concern us are the constant emphasis upon things, and the universal assumption of modern man that "better living" means having more comfort and pleasure and more of the things which induce comfort and pleasure. The whole force of technological genius has served to sell people the conviction that their "most priceless possessions" can be stored in a little box in the sub-basement of a bank and that the supreme aim of life is to satisfy one's desires in as poignant a way and over as long a period of time as possible. Power, in a scientific epoch, means physical power, in terms of health, sex, and wealth for the individual, and food, money, and atomic weapons of defense for the nation.[19] Simultaneously, in the ever-increasing demand for security, the security that the individual and the nation really calls for is a physical security. For what the individual demands—as the leaders of the Western nations so shrewdly know—is a government which will give him adequate housing, sufficient food, constant employment, and motherly care from "his cradle to his grave." For man's condition beyond the grave there is no concern yet. Nor is the philosophy of national

[19] See in this connection *Endless Horizons* by Vannevar Bush (Washington, D. C.: Public Affairs Press, 1946).

as contrasted with individual security fundamentally different, for it is largely measured in terms of the physical capacity of the nation to maintain and defend itself and "the American standard of living." Is this, then, the "American Prayer"?:

> I believe in Advertising almighty,
> And the power and the glory
> Of the ten-engine, streamlined, supersonic
> Method of getting from here to nowhere.
> I believe in the trinity
> Of Gush, Mush and Slush.
> Help me to celebrate worthily
> The holy festival of Dollar Day.
> Clothe me in the form-fitting,
> Peerless, sheer, nonshrink
> Garments of righteousness.
> Anoint my face
> With Magic Mirror Cream,
> Making every wrinkle
> Vanish in a twinkle.
> Almighty Advertising,
> Give us this day
> Our cloud-soft, Puff-quick Biscuits,
> And the tangy, bangy goodness
> of crusty Crackle-crunch.
> Forgive us the debts on our easy payments,
> And that time we wore the wrong hat.
> May the incense of our prayer
> Rise through a cough-free filter,
> And the cool-refreshing dews of Sparkle-juice
> Slake our every desire.
> In the hour of our death
> May we rest on a feather-soft,
> Mother-soft Marvel Mattress,
> And drift into the cosy rosy dozey
> Of Rock-a-bye Land. Amen.[20]

[20] Edith Lovejoy Pierce, *The Christian Century* (June 29, 1955), p. 752.

ANTI-INTELLECTUALISM

Any effort to interpret the characteristics of the modern mind would be incomplete and inaccurate if it failed to take into consideration the recent wave of anti-intellectualism in the Western world. To understand what this is and why it occurs, one must, as usual, see it in its relation to the dominant beliefs which were forming for over two hundred years—from the Enlightenment, if not indeed from the Renaissance. The cluster of ideas and values which we inherit, and which still survive in present-day culture, are those of the triumph of reason. We inherit the belief in the capacity of man, if only he will use his reason and scientific techniques skilfully enough, to solve most of his individual and collective problems. We retain the conviction that, in spite of certain shocking slips and retreats, the human race is surely progressing, that democracy is clearly the most advanced form of human government—in short, that optimism is warranted regarding man and his status in a universe which he is increasingly comprehending and mastering. Although it is true that among the intellectuals there have been isolated voices of cynicism and despair and warners of impending doom, they either were not widely heard or, if heard, were shrugged off as cultural misfits, blowing a false note at the wrong time. Witness Kierkegaard, Nietzsche, and Spengler.

In our own age, however, a newer and stronger characteristic has appeared which for want of a better word must be called anti-intellectualism. This may mean two things: hostility to reason and glorification of the irrational or nonrational, or a serious effort to discover the actual role of reason and of rational processes in human life. It is inaccurate and dangerous to confuse these two meanings of "anti-intellectual." The former is voiced by the poets, Goethe, Wordsworth, and others who ridicule pale and lifeless rationalists—asserting that "feeling is all." It often goes much farther, as in Nietzsche or Hitler, who cry out for us to think with our blood.

Those who understand irrationalism in the second sense are not given to these wild outbursts. They seek more judiciously to discover the actual role of reason in human affairs and, in so doing, conclude that non-rational factors play a much more determining role than the children of the Enlightenment imagined. The curious fact is that whereas the anti-intellectual is on the face of it opposed to the beliefs of the typical modern Western spokesman (such a belief, for example, that by use of education and the scientific techniques all people can eventually be taught to think and act well), he ultimately is a believer that his case must be made reasonably and that thought can improve man's lot. A few representative figures will illustrate our main point. Note, however, that we are not here evaluating the method used by the persons we are studying, but are concerned with their larger and over-all influence upon the thought and life of their fellowmen.

One such figure is Sigmund Freud, and it is of interest that he worked in a science which was so new that in many of the leading institutions in America it (psychology) was considered until this generation a subdivision of philosophy. The positivistic background of Freud's work, his pessimism regarding metaphysics, and his effort to make the highly-suspect psychoanalysis a solid and respected part of medical science are all complications in the way of assessing his influence on the present century. Yet the basic respect in which he represents anti-intellectualism can be said to be this: He, like Pavlov and others, placed great emphasis upon those portions of human action which are not determined by the intellect or reason but chiefly, if not solely, by non-rational factors. Action, as the anti-intellectualist came to believe, is largely the result of conditioned responses, unconscious urges and drives (such as what he first called the libido and later the id), and even social and religious habits and predispositions which condition the individual from earliest childhood. "To the anti-intellectualist, actual ratiocinative thought in an individual is to the rest of his living even less than the small part of the iceberg visible above the water is to the whole mass of the iceberg. The amount of reasoning in human life, then, and not the existence of reasoning, is the point over which the anti-intellectual and those who oppose anti-intellectualism really differ. The tradition of American moral and political thinking is not anti-intellectual. The practice of a good deal of American politics, and of much of American life—advertising is a clear example—is anti-intellectual." [21]

Other representatives of anti-intellectualism can be cited to show how, from different points of view, each makes his attack upon reason in the name of this or that alleged set of facts or considerations. Thus, Nietzsche attacked the moral ground of nineteenth-century assumptions and strenuously advocated the cause of the superman as one who by power and use of will makes truths rather than, like a pale intellectual, merely contemplates truth. Men, Nietzsche informed his readers in pseudo-biblical writings, often achieve their goals by acting on what to reason are erroneous ideas. In this same general mood, Pareto, the engineer-mathematician and formerly ideal scholar turned sociologist became a disillusioned liberal, turning farther and farther from belief in individual liberty, democracy, international peace, the sharing of ideas, and the like, until in *The Mind and Society* and other works he can argue that at bottom the deeply ingrained habits of human beings, resting in our biological nature, are more powerful and even more useful in the survival of a people than are the endless intellectual arguments of the believers in sweet reason. Thus, finally, Kierkegaard, reacting against the Hegelian emphasis upon the logical procedures for grasping truth by reason, and attacking the religious ground of the nineteenth-century idealism, argued that in the genuinely ultimate concerns—one's very

[21] Crain Brinton, *Ideas and Men* (New York: Prentice-Hall, 1950), p. 513.

existence—not reason but a paradoxical leap of faith in the face of reason is the mark of religious stature.

So we see that in the midst of the emphasis upon critical intelligence and the scientific method, voices were eloquently raised within the fields of psychology, sociology, ethics, politics, and religion, claiming that the nonintellectual factors are and should be the determining ones in the good life. One more influence— the German, Karl Marx—completes what I should like to call the volcanic influences on the late nineteenth-century and early twentieth-century Western world. For, as Kierkegaard threatened its religious grounds, Nietzsche its moral ground, so Marx's eruptive volcano threatened the economico-political ground of the presumed synthesis.[22]

The Western world has yet to adjust theoretically and practically to these volcanic actions. About some of these influential voices, it would like to think it has made its decision. The ideas of Pareto and Nietzsche have been largely rejected, but the voices of Freud and Kierkegaard have grown stronger in the middle of the twentieth century. No effort to interpret the mind of the Western world today is complete if it fails to place this troublesome issue centrally in its portrait.[23]

[22] See Paul Tillich, "The Present Theological Situation in the Light of Continental European Development," *Theology Today*, VI, 3 (October 1949), p. 2.

[23] Sigmund Freud *Introductory Lectures on Psychoanalysis*, trans. G. I. Riviere (New York: Garden City Books, 1943), p. 240, expresses forcefully what we have been discussing:

"Humanity has in the course of time had to endure from the hands of science two great outrages upon its naive self-love. The first was when it realized that our earth was not the centre of the universe, but only a tiny speck in the world-system. . . . That is associated in our minds with the name of Copernicus. . . . The second was when biological research robbed man of his peculiar privilege of having been specially created, and relegated him to a descent from the animal world, implying an ineradicable animal nature in him; this transvaluation has been accomplished in our time upon the instigation of Charles Darwin, Wallace and their predecessors. . . . But man's craving for grandiosity is now suffering the third and most bitter blow from the present day psychological research, which is endeavoring to prove to the "ego" of each one of us that he is not even master in his own

INDIVIDUALISM VS. COLLECTIVISM

Closely related to the appearance of anti-intellectualism in the thought and life of the Western world has been the growing tension in recent decades between individualism and collectivism. Our world outlook is, on the one hand, strongly individualistic: Americans have always loved liberty and conceived of it in very personal and practical terms. The roots of individualism are also partly in the Renaissance, described so aptly by John Addington Symonds as "the discovery of the world and the rediscovery of man." These roots are also religious. They come from the New Testament and the Reformation, as in Luther's doctrines of the priesthood of all believers, the right of individual conscience, and the obligation of universal education for religious and political citizenship—though men did not talk then of "individualism." The two centuries following the Reformation saw what was involved, and by the twentieth century they did talk of individualism—in economic, political, social, indeed of all the areas of human relations. Whatever else our Western tradition has been, it is firmly individualistic.

This, however, is not the whole truth. In the present half-century, there have arisen new and powerful anti-individualistic and anti-libertarian forces. Perhaps the most obvious, and to some the most terrifying of these forces, have appeared in the political sphere. Our century has witnessed the philosophies of statism and political collectivism—Japanese, Italian, and German nationalism, and Russian political collectivism—which stand radically opposed to belief in individualism, democracy, and liberty. A whole chapter could be written here to show how these collectivisms grasp the claims of anti-intellectualism to advance the aim of the group—nation, church, and people. In combating such forces, even those who most cherish the democratic individualism

house but that he must remain content with the barest scraps of information about what is going on unconsciously in his own mind."

we have known often plead that in war and in times like ours, we simply must have more authority, more collectivism, and less individualism, less liberty.

In the social as in the political sphere, we witness the appearance of a crowd culture, a deadly tendency to uniformity. The effects of this on the thinking and habits of people are described in other chapters. In the economic realm, the shift from individualism to collectivism is so manifest as to require no delineation. In the citadel of the Western democracies, the United States, it would be difficult today to find a forthright defender of economic individualism in the sense that phrase was used among capitalists during the three previous centuries. In saying this, we are not pronouncing judgment but describing factors in the mentality of the West. Individualism is not dead, any more than is our conviction that, given the opportunity of education, the rationality of the common man can be trusted.[24] The attacks on both sets of assumptions, however, are made more frequently and insistently.

WAR VS. INTERNATIONAL LAW

No analysis of the contemporary cultural situation can be adequate if it fails to take into account the threat of modern war and the ideal of international law. The specific issues involved have been treated and mistreated in millions of spoken and written words by everyone from the executives of the American Association for Advancement of Science to wild-eyed evangelists of apocalyptic-minded religious sects. All agree, amazingly, that the question of the use of the hydrogen bomb and guided missiles is the life or death issue of Western civilization. Three problems which require analysis are the following:

First, the problem of modern warfare is a dramatic, terrifying documentation of the accuracy of our contention that the leit-

[24] See David Riesman, *Individualism Reconsidered* (Glencoe, Ill.: Free Press, 1955).

motif of our epoch is science and that its product is a "mass-man" with a sense of utter helplessness. The fear which grips the heart of every modern man that hydrogen warfare will suddenly strike its fatal blow is without question the direct fruit, in part, of science. Our epoch, therefore, has in one respect come the full circle around: That to which man looked for his material salvation has become the source of what he now realizes can produce complete annihilation.[25]

Second, the leading exponents of scientific method, frightened by the prospect of sudden collective annihilation, often exhibit a religious zeal in their effort to warn people against the destructive use of their discoveries. Put it this way: Modern science is working overtime to devise ways of saving us from the devices of modern science. Professor J. C. Philip, former president of the Chemical Section of the British Association for the Advancement of Science, writes:

Scientists (are) increasingly impatient at the extent to which their knowledge is made to serve inhuman ends. . . . Impelled by patriotic motives, most scientists have put themselves freely at the disposal of the state and admit that patriotism must always override considerations of humanity. . . . Whatever be our individual attitude in this matter, it is time for chemists and scientists in general to throw their weight into the scales against the tendencies now dragging science and civilization down and debasing our heritage of intellectual and spiritual values.[26]

We have purposely quoted this twenty-year-old statement for three reasons. For one thing, it shows that more than three years

[25] So strong a statement may, in the minds of some readers, require documentation. This exists in such abundance that I should mention only a few, notably, the "statement" by 12 leading atomic scientists, made public February 5, 1952 (and published that date in *The New York Times*) at the time of the meeting of the American Physical Society at Columbia University. See also E. P. Wigner, *Physical Science and Human Values* (Princeton: Princeton Univ. Press, 1948).

[26] Quoted by Paul F. Laubenstein in "The Moral Price of Science," *The Christian Century* (December 9, 1936), pp. 1653-4.

before the Second World War, the better scientific minds saw the handwriting on the wall and correctly read its meaning. For another thing, they saw the inseparable connection between the issues of scientific freedom of inquiry and ethical values generally. Last, and most important, they now appear to be more terrified and less competent to halt the use of their techniques of destruction than ever before. They are even taking the first steps of retrenchment in relinquishing the universal use of their methodology and becoming the servants of particular national or political groups. For example, Dr. Lloyd V. Berkner proposed that our government, in the present international situation, have a scientist with diplomatic rank attached to all our important embassies. These men would be charged to keep American science informed of every important scientific development abroad.[27] Such a proposal shows that the scientists are politically as well as personally involved.

To an earlier generation of scientists, this proposal would have been astounding for two reasons. First, it runs counter to the proud claim of the scientists to be genuinely international. Scientific advance in medicine, for example, has generally been reported promptly to every other country. The laboratories of the world and the fruit of their research stood open with few exceptions to any accredited scientist regardless of race, nation or religion. Moreover, scientists would have been surprised at such a proposal because of its practical effect. Would it not place them in the embarrassing position of appearing to the Russians, for example, as little more than superspies? When "science" is a pigeonhole of an embassy, and its workers have diplomatic immunity, what has become of the open, shared, universal quest for truth?

The third and final problem we face here, as in earlier portions of our analysis, is a fundamental contradiction in the "mind" of

[27] See "Should Scientists Have Diplomatic Status?" (editorial), *The Christian Century* (June 21, 1950), p. 748.

Western civilization. The deep-seated dilemma is that our age is at once the most destructive (in fact and in possibility) and the potentially most constructive in human history. Each half of this dilemma can be briefly documented as follows.

Professor Quincy Wright has summarized the fact that European powers alone fought seventy-four wars during the first thirty years of our century. From the eleventh to the twentieth centuries, he tells us, war casualties totaled roughly eighteen million. In the first thirty years of our century, we killed 33 1/3 per cent more persons than were killed in the previous eight hundred years. And these figures do not include World War II. Thus, the following statement by Dean Howard M. Jones of the Harvard Graduate School comes to a conclusion which everyone can understand.

If any human being brought up in the tradition of western civilization could, by some miracle, step outside the familiar patterns of that culture; if history could come to him with the same shock of surprise that a new and stimulating novel brings him; if, in sum, retaining the moral idealism of western civilization as a standard of measurement, he could yet discover for the first time what has happened to mankind in the last fifty years, such a person would, I think, be overwhelmed by a single tragic conviction; namely, that the history of mankind for the last half century has been a history of deepening horror. . . .

If the entire population of the United States were wiped out tomorrow, their number would be less than the number of human beings who have died of violence, disease, or starvation in war or as a result of it during the last half century. It doesn't make sense.[28]

The other half of this dilemma in the mind of Western civilization is dramatically captured in a statement by Arnold Toynbee that the twentieth century will be remembered chiefly as an age in which human society dared to think of the welfare of the whole human race as a practicable objective. Puzzling as it may seem,

[28] Howard Lowry, *The Mind's Adventure* (Philadelphia: Westminster Press, 1950), pp. 17-18.

our age has the dawning realization that mankind as a whole has claims upon our loyalty which can be met only by a United Nations acting co-operatively under law.

The purpose of our study has been served if this analysis of the contemporary mind has achieved its aim of comprehension and diagnosis, not prescription. We have pointed to dilemmas and tensions, not to proposed remedies or solutions. One conclusion is plain: The mind of our age is a divided one. Science, and the fruits of science, have given us the ability to satisfy the basic physical needs of all mankind, but they have also given us the capacity for collective self-destruction and such terror of its likelihood that we enjoy neither individual peace of mind nor international security. The second half of the twentieth century will witness the resolution of this tension in a way no one can now predict.

BIBLIOGRAPHY

There is a considerable amount of literature devoted to an interpretation of the mind of our age. Moreover, so much is of good quality that it is impossible to select a few books and pronounce them the best. The following are among the best:

Beard, Charles A., *America in Midpassage* (New York: Macmillan Co., 1939)

Brinton, Crain., *Ideas and Men* (New York: Prentice-Hall, 1950)

Dewey, John, *A Common Faith* (New Haven: Yale Univ. Press, 1934)

Frank, Phillip, *Philosophy of Science* (Englewood Cliffs, N. J.: Prentice-Hall, Inc., 1957)

Fromm, Erich, *Escape from Freedom* (New York: Rinehart & Co., 1941)

Harkness, Georgia, *Secularism, The Modern Rival of Christian Faith* (New York: Abingdon-Cokesbury, 1952)

Hocking, W. E., *Science and the Idea of God* (Chapel Hill: Univ. of North Carolina Press, 1944)

Hutchison, John A. (ed.) *Christian Faith and Social Action* (New York: Charles Scribner's Sons, 1953)

Northrop, F. S. C., *The Meeting of East and West* (New York: Macmillan Co., 1946)

Parrington, V. L., *Main Currents in American Thought* (3 vols.; New York: Harcourt Brace and Co., 1927)

Randall, John H., Sr., *The Making of the Modern Mind* (Boston: Houghton Mifflin Co., 1940)

Sorokin, Pitirim, *Social Philosophies in an Age of Crisis* (Boston: Beacon Press, 1950)

Tillich, Paul, *The Protestant Era* (Chicago: Univ. of Chicago Press, 1948)

_____. *The Religious Situation*, trans. H. R. Niebuhr (New York: Henry Holt and Co., 1932)

Toynbee, Arnold, *A Study of History* (New York: Oxford Univ. Press, 1935-1954)

Whitehead, A. N., *Science and the Modern World* (New York: Macmillan Co., 1927)

Wilder, Amos, (ed.), *Liberal Learning and Religion* (New York: Harper & Bros., 1951)

CHAPTER 3

Personal Life in an Age of Anxiety

by Franklin Sherman

"The schism in the body social," writes Arnold Toynbee at a major transition point in his monumental *A Study of History*, "is a collective experience and therefore superficial. Its significance lies in its being the outward and visible sign of an inward and spiritual rift." Under the title "Schism in the Soul," Toynbee then proceeds to analyze the psychological dimension of the breakdown and disintegration of civilizations.[1]

Regardless of the extent to which we are willing to accept this historian's particular schematization of "the pattern of the past," we must acknowledge the cogency of his thus linking the inner nuances of the spirit with the outer dramas of social, cultural, political, and economic history. For we have learned from our own experience in the contemporary world that the travail of a "civilization in transition" cannot but deeply affect the personal lives of the men and women whose joint endeavors constitute that civilization.

At times when relative tranquillity prevails upon the social scene, it is easy for the individual to assume that he is fully "captain of his soul"—that he is free (within the limits, to be sure, of his biological inheritance) to fashion his own character and choose his destiny. Thus even the new discipline of psychology,

[1] Arnold Toynbee, *A Study of History*, D. C. Somervell abridgement (New York: Oxford Univ. Press, 1947), pp. 429 ff.

as it emerged in the nineteenth and early twentieth centuries, could consider a procedure "scientific" that lifted the single individual completely out of his societal milieu, whether for study in the laboratory or for therapy in the consulting room. Likewise, the Protestant churches in their pietistic phase, while possessed of a far deeper understanding of individuality than the contemporary secular culture, regrettably narrowed the focus of their insight by neglecting the socio-cultural dimension.

But at a time such as our own when the tempests of social ferment blow so exceeding strong that the stoutest craft of self-reliance seems a frail bark before the tide, we are more ready to attend to the intimate connection between inner and outer history. Whether it be among the general populace, in the intensifying of the elders' perhaps perennial lament over the "lost generation"; or among the scholars, forced to recast their framework of interpretation and revise their estimate of human possibilities; or among the creative artists, or those responsible for political decisions, there is a heightened sensitivity to the implications for personal life of the vast historic drama in which we are engaged. And so the churches, too, take up with a new urgency their social responsibility, finding their ministry to persons inadequate without co-ordinate concern for the community enveloping those persons.

The very terms "person" and "personality" are suggestive of this emphasis, derived as they are via the Latin *persona* from the Greek word signifying the mask worn by the actor in the classic theatre, and thereby the dramatic role he played. Social psychology can view the personality as consisting in a concatenation of such "roles" played by the individual, both in his intimate relationships and in the larger social institutions. Likewise, social philosophy can appropriate this distinction in moving from an atomistic individualism toward recognition of the vital function of smaller communities within the whole, as in Jacques Maritain's call for a "democracy of the person" rather than a "democracy

of the individual." [2] Yet no re-emphasis upon the social condition-
ing of personal existence should be permitted to obscure the final
uniqueness and creative freedom that make it impossible fully to
comprehend any single human life within a sociological scheme.[3]

In truth the relationship between the self and the community,
as Reinhold Niebuhr has reiterated in a recent formulation, is a
complex one. From one perspective, the self stands "below" the
community which is the source and sustainer of its existence, both
physical and psychical. On the plane of historical encounters
between groups, however, the self stands "with" its community,
identifying itself with its own as against alternative communities.
But in the perspective of eternity, and by virtue of its direct
relationship to the transcendent, the self stands "above" all groups
and communities.[4]

Similarly complex is the individual's relation to the "culture"
which may be said to provide the content, as "society" provides
the form, of his interconnection with the community. We are
using "culture," of course, not to refer to the fine arts, but in its
broader anthropological meaning of "the sum total of ideas,
conditioned emotional responses, and patterns of habitual behavior which the members of [a given] society have acquired
through instruction or imitation and which they share to a
greater or less degree." [5] Surely it is individual men and women
who are ultimately responsible for the origin, continuation, and
transmittal of a culture, even though their action may be in

[2] Jacques Maritain, *The Person and the Common Good* (New York:
Charles Scribner's Sons, 1947).

[3] Cognizance is taken of this truth within the best contemporary social
psychology, especially that stemming from the work of George Herbert
Mead, who distinguished the unpredictable and private "I" from the socially-
determined "me." Cf. his *Mind, Self, and Society* (Chicago: Univ. of
Chicago Press, 1934).

[4] Reinhold Niebuhr, *The Self and the Dramas of History* (New York:
Charles Scribner's Sons, 1955), pp. 35 ff.

[5] Ralph Linton, *The Study of Man* (New York: Appleton-Century-
Crofts, 1936), p. 288.

concert, or in part unconscious. Culture, as man's creation of a "secondary environment," is the embodiment of individuals' persistent search for meaning in existence: in daily language as well as in great symbolic systems, in common custom as in the broad traditions of a people, culture incarnates the fruits of man's struggle both to comprehend and to reshape his world. Yet to any particular individual, or even to an entire generation, the inherited ways of thinking, feeling, and behaving, together with the given symbols, institutions, and technologies, constitute so powerfully formative a factor that man seems as much the creature as the creator of his culture. But only "to a greater or less degree," as even the anthropologist must recognize.

Thus in discussing the impact upon personal life of large scale historic trends, we cannot expect to depict with exactitude the character of any specific individual. At best we can provide some insight into what Erich Fromm has termed the "social character" —"the essential nucleus of the character structure of most members of a group which has developed as the result of the basic experiences and mode of life common to that group." [6] Within the vast expanse of Western civilization, there are of course a multitude of such environing communities, and many subcultures within the common cultural frame. Even within the limits of American society, which is the principal focus of discussion in the present chapter, the diversity of life patterns among regions, classses, occupations, and nationality and racial groups remains so great as to require deliberate abstraction and generalization if common traits of culture and of character are to be discerned.

THE AMERICAN MOOD

"What then is the American, this new man?" queried that early interpreter, the French emigré Michel-Guillaume de Crèvecoeur, who during the decade of the Revolutionary War addressed to

[6] Erich Fromm, *Escape from Freedom* (New York: Rinehart & Co., 1941), p. 277.

his former countrymen the pseudonymous *Letters from an American Farmer*. "*He* is an American, who, leaving behind him all his ancient prejudices and manners, receives new ones from the new mode of life he has embraced, the new government he obeys, and the new rank he holds." Crèvecoeur's faithfulness to the exuberant mood of his adopted land is well reflected in his affirmation: "We are the most perfect society now existing in the world." [7]

For if faith in the infinite possibilities of the development of man and society toward the envisioned good be listed as a central characteristic of modern Western man, it is *a fortiori* an American trait. The American's own experience of conquering a virgin continent, combined with the enthusiasm of his "great experiment" in democracy, fortified the already optimistic aspects of the eighteenth century's confidence in reason, and the following century's faith in evolution or in progress. Ralph Waldo Emerson, celebrant of the goodness of the human soul and of the self-reliant individual, might well be taken as the typical figure of the American culture of that period, as in fact he was a dominant influence in it.

Against this background, how striking a contrast is offered by the mood of disillusionment and dismay that has become endemic in the life and literature of our own time. The current search for "peace of mind" and the pathetic eagerness of many people even for the most superficial pseudo-religious reassurances, as well as the more genuine evidences of religious renewal, mark but the latest outcropping of a deep-seated spiritual malaise whose growth within our culture can be traced back at least to the First World War. T. S. Eliot's *The Waste Land* (1922) was perhaps the first literary creation to attain the status of a universal symbol for this mood of despair, and Eliot has remained in his later poetry and drama an eloquent spokesman for the perplexities of contemporary man. The novels of F. Scott Fitzgerald gave

[7] Quoted in *America in Perspective*, ed. Henry Steele Commager (New York: New American Library, 1947), pp. 23, 21.

poignant expression to the ennui of "all the sad young men," as the early Hemingway reflected the moral rootlessness of that "Jazz Age" generation. In the thirties came the Great Depression to flatten not only the American economy but the American soul; and then descended the equally unexpected shock of another and far more terrible war, followed not by peace but by another full decade of world crisis and revolutionary upheaval.

In such circumstances it was understandable that sensitive individuals quite representative of our society, and not necessarily especially neurotic, should begin to show manifestations of that "catastrophic expectation" which has been defined by psychologists as the fundamental constellation in mental illness. When the individual encounters in his environment some factor that seems to constitute a profound threat to his own security, he may experience an intense "expectation of abandonment, injury and annihilation, condemnation and disapproval, humiliation, enslavement, loss of love, and utter deprivation." Accompanying this expectation, we are told, is a "self-devaluation" of equal intensity —an utter loss of self-esteem.[8] It is this connection between self and environment that one of Scott Fitzgerald's characters expressed, with unusually gentle cynicism, when he said, "The world is so overgrown that it can't lift its own fingers, and I was planning to be such an important finger." The same is true of the pathetic figure of Willy Loman in *Death of a Salesman;* and the deep impression that this drama has made, on both stage and screen, is perhaps due in no small part to the large number of Americans who secretly identified themselves with Willy's disillusion and despair. The preoccupation with psychic and social degeneracy, violence, and horror in American literature of the twentieth century, in contrast with the preceding age of literary innocence, indeed lends credence to Pascal's remark:

[8] A. H. Maslow and Bela Mittelman, *Principles of Abnormal Psychology: The Dynamics of Psychic Illness* (2nd ed.; New York: Harper & Bros., 1951), pp. 72 ff.

"Man either hides his miseries, or, if he disclose them, glories in knowing them."

The revised contemporary estimate of the leading representatives of America's literary past is itself a sign of our own time. Now not Ralph Waldo Emerson, but his then unheralded contemporary Herman Melville appears to be the giant of the nineteenth century: Melville, the spokesman for the ambiguity and the tragedy of life, who in *Moby Dick* created a classic image of the powerful, irrational, and evil forces against which man carries on his endless but unavailing struggle. Likewise has recent criticism renewed its appreciation for such a profound interpreter of the psychology of evil as Nathaniel Hawthorne, as well as that master of morbidity, Edgar Allen Poe.

But of all American literary creations, perhaps none has proved more expressive of the mood of the present generation (as Eliot's *The Waste Land* did thirty years ago), than W. H. Auden's book-length dramatic poem, *The Age of Anxiety*. For it is probably not specific fears, whether personal or social, that are wreaking the deepest psychic havoc in contemporary life, but this "nameless and faceless *dread*," or anxiety—the haunting sense of an irretrievably misspent past, an empty present, and a hostile future. So many of us share the plight of Auden's foursome brooding at the bar:

> Self-judged they sit,
> Sad haunters of Perhaps who after years
> To grasp and gaze in have got no further
> Than their first beholding . . .

And those whose entire lives have been set within this troubled century know with especial intimacy all the varieties of futility that Auden records in his new version of the "seven ages of man"; so that their feeling would correspond with that of his discouraged company:

Whether they thought of Nature, of her unending stream of irrelevant events without composition or center, her reckless waste of value, her alternate looks of idiotic inertia and insane ferocity, or whether they thought of Man, of the torpor of his spirit, the indigent dryness of his soul, his bottomless credulity, his perverse preference for the meretricious or the insipid—it seemed impossible to them that either could have survived so long had not some semi-divine stranger with superhuman powers, some Gilgamesh or Napoleon, some Solon or Sherlock Holmes, appeared from time to time to rescue both, for a brief bright instant, from their egregious destructive blunders.

Yet, Auden continues, so deeply entrenched is modern man's illusion of his own autonomy that man finds himself unwilling, even before his authentic Lord, to yield up his disbelief:

> Wanting our own way, unwilling to say Yes
> To the Self-So which is the same at all times,
> That Always-Opposite which is the whole subject
> Of our not-knowing, yet from no necessity
> Condescended to exist and to suffer death
> And, scorned on a scaffold, ensconced in His life
> The human household. In our anguish we struggle
> To elude Him, to lie to Him, yet His love observes
> His appalling promise; His predilection
> As we wander and weep is with us to the end.[9]

RIVAL DIAGNOSES

That man's experience in the contemporary world has increasingly been accompanied by the overtones of anguish can hardly be denied by the sensitive participant-observer. In specific diagnosis of our present plight, however, there has been wide divergence. Not all, by any means, would agree with Auden's implication that our malaise may be due most basically to man's flight from God.

[9] W. H. Auden, *The Age of Anxiety* (London: Faber and Faber, Ltd., 1948), pp. 16, 97, 125. The poem already has inspired a symphony of the same title by Leonard Bernstein, as well as a ballet based on the poem and the symphony.

Many, in fact, would take the opposite view, attributing man's psychic burden precisely to the survival, in a presumably emancipated age, of "irrational" religious attitudes, especially the attitude of self-condemnation before a "judgmental" and "authoritarian" divinity. Once overthrow these totems and taboos, according to these interpreters, and man will at last be freed for self-fulfilment.

Such has clearly been the theory of one major stream of thought in our century, the "classic" school of psychoanalysis directly dependent on Sigmund Freud. In the Freudian view, there dwells within every man a brood of libidinous desires, of either a sexual or an aggressive character (or both), which clamor to be satisfied. Our culture, however, according to this diagnosis, forbids the overt satisfaction of such impulses; therefore, they must be repressed into the subconscious. Yet they continue to press upon the threshold of the conscious mind; and it is this pressure which results in the feeling of anxiety. Though the individual cannot identify its source, the anxiety actually represents the tension between his desires and his apprehension of the punishment which would result if he were to express them. Anxiety is the precipitate of the perpetual struggle of the "superego" to repress the "id"— the id (Latin for "it") being the seat of the instinctive drives, and the superego or conscience serving as the inner censor on behalf of a religiously- or culturally-sanctioned moralism. This censor is created during the early years of life by the child's "introjection" of parental demands, and by his "identification" with a powerful father-figure. Given this analysis of the situation, psychotherapy then logically consists in freeing the individual from his irrational bondage to a rigid conscience.

The extent to which our culture has been penetrated by this understanding of the human problem may be illustrated by certain developments in family relationships, especially with respect to patterns of training of the child.

Throughout its history, the Western family has been of what

the anthropologist would call the "conjugal" rather than the "extended" type. This is to say that, unlike certain other cultures in which a large number of both male and female relatives are included in the basic unit, the family in our society comprises simply the mother, father, and immediate offspring. Particularly in America, the ideal of "every family in a home of its own" requires the establishment of a new social unit with every marriage. Thus cut off from close ties either horizontally to a larger kinship unit, or vertically to the foregoing generation (both of which cleavages are especially accentuated in a mobile and urbanized environment), the conjugal family finds that its own intimate relationships are invested with a peculiar emotional intensity, of immense significance for psychic good or harm.

Within this persisting framework there have occurred during the past fifty years vast changes in the Western family, attributable to both ideological and social forces. Here we cannot discuss the full range of these developments, but are concerned primarily with the revolt against the predominantly patriarchal character of the traditional family, a revolt that has been aided and abetted by Freudian influences. The unquestioned authority of the father has been destroyed, and his power dissipated. The ideal of "self-expression" has replaced former standards of strict discipline. Parents have been encouraged to be "permissive" rather than "punitive"; and, in general, we have experienced an era of family "democracy," of "accent on the child."

One unusually keen observer has pointed out that the typical pattern of American family relationships seems to embody not only the broad notion of democracy, but also leading features of the distinctively American governmental system of checks and balances. In the British parliamentary system, the government is organized in hierarchical fashion under a definite locus of final responsibility and power; and the party that at any one time holds possession of that power must be united in policy. This arrangement seems to correspond to the traditional family pattern, in which both the establishment of policy and the power to enforce it are firmly vested in the father. In the American government, on the other hand, policy making has no single locus, but proceeds by means of a continually changing balance of power among the legislative, executive, and judicial structures (as well as the pressure groups); and the political parties represent not clearly articulated ideologies, but congeries of special interests only partially resolved. So in the American "democratic" family, power is shared by all, and each member of the family represents not so much a specific role, qualitatively defined, but a certain quantity of influence entering into the balance-of-power relationship through which decisions are made. As in the corresponding governmental system, a constant process of change, correction, and self-regulation by all elements is implied.[10]

No doubt this represents improvement in some respects over a harshly authoritarian family regime; but the question arises whether the normal child really is prepared to enter into such a flexible relationship. Those concerned with family counseling and child guidance, as well as sensitive parents themselves, have increasingly been asking whether the child does not have a deep-seated need precisely for dependence, for rather definite guidance, and for strong parental images over against which he can establish his own identity. Jurgen Ruesch has pointed out how confusing it can be to a young mind when "in the father's voice there are overtones of the mother's sentiments; and in the mother's voice when she addresses the child there are overtones of agreement with the child." [11] His opportunity for discovering either his own or his parents' individuality is blurred. After several decades of experience with the permissive approach, it is noteworthy that psychiatrists report no decline in the incidence of

[10] Jurgen Ruesch, "Communication and the System of Checks and Balances," in Jurgen Ruesch and Gregory Bateson, *Communication: The Social Matrix of Psychiatry* (New York: W. W. Norton and Co., 1951).

[11] *Ibid.,* p. 164.

neurotic tendencies either in children or adults; if anything, the opposite is the case. They report only that the form of the problem has changed: rather than symptoms of repression or rigidity, patients today typically manifest so-called "character disturbances" which seem to center in a *lack* of conscience and self-control. No matter how democratic the relationship between parent and child might be, the child still must form the rudiments of his own self-identity on the basis of the image that the parent presents. But this means that he internalizes the indecisiveness of the permissive parent and the unsolved conflicts of the equalitarian family relationship, as much as he did the explicit standards of the more authoritarian pattern.[12]

The child himself has seemed to show that he has a basic need for limits as well as liberty, and that the exercise of discipline by the parents is necessary not merely for their convenience, but for the child's own security and character formation. Parents have realized that if by virtue of their allegiance to "progressive" notions of child care they fail to provide such a framework, they have failed both the child himself and the society with the transmittal of whose cultural heritage they are charged. In this connection, it is interesting to note the recent reaction also against many of the consequences of the "emancipation of women" from male dominance and from the confines of the home. Appreciative of her new privileges but confused as to her real identity, and fearful lest her femininity may have been lost, the modern career woman seems in process of returning to the home and family.

Among those who have taken these developments most seriously is the research psychologist O. H. Mowrer, who maintains (in contradiction to the Freudian view) that it is not repression of the id but *repression of the superego* that lies at the root of

[12] Cf. Theresa Benedek, "The Emotional Structure of the Family," in *The Family: Its Function and Destiny*, ed. Ruth Nanda Anshen (New York: Harper and Bros., 1949).

typical present-day anxiety. In most instances, Mowrer notes, "neurotics present a history of more rather than less self-indulgence than does the average person. . . . Neurotics are persons who are ethically stunted." They suffer not from biological but from moral frustration. Terming his a "guilt theory" rather than an "impulse theory" of anxiety, Mowrer concludes: "Anxiety comes, not from acts which the individual would commit but dares not, but from acts which he has committed but wishes he had not." [13]

In the legend created by Friedrich Nietzsche, it is a "madman" who appears on the streets and in his frenzy cries out, "God is dead!" Yet he is not so mad that he fails to sense the truly monstrous consequences of that proclamation—and his words now strike us not as fable but as realistic comment on the travail of our own anxious age:

We have killed him—you and I. All of us are his murderers. But how have we done this? How were we able to drink up the sea? Who gave us the sponge to wipe away the entire horizon? What did we do when we unchained this earth from its sun? . . . Are we not plunging continually? Backward, sideward, forward, in all directions? Is there any up or down left? Are we not straying as through an infinite nothing? Do we not feel the breath of empty space? Has it not become colder? Is not night and more night coming on all the while?[14]

[12] O. Herbart Mowrer, *Learning Theory and Personality Dynamics* (New York: Ronald Press, 1950), pp. 462, 537. The foregoing remarks should not be interpreted to imply that there is no truth at all in the Freudian position. There is undoubtedly a perennial element of repressive moralism in the human psyche—an element particularly dominant in the Victorian culture in which psychoanalysis first flourished. But the problem of our own emancipated generation seems more nearly to be that of those who are indeed "free from the law," but have used their freedom "as an opportunity for the flesh" (Gal. 5:13).

[14] *The Portable Nietzsche*, trans. and ed. Walter Kaufman (New York: Viking Press, 1954), p. 95.

SOCIAL SOURCES OF ANXIETY

Not only, however, has the modern individual experienced emancipation from moral discipline and religious faith; he likewise has been released from his ancestral social bonds. Both developments, though temporarily exhilarating, have proved in the long run a source of suffering. As Martin Buber has observed, our age has been an "epoch of homelessness" in a double sense— cosmic homelessness and social homelessness. Neither dimension dare be neglected in an analysis of the predicament of modern man.

In the medieval order, Burckhardt reminds us, "man was conscious of himself only as a member of a race, people, party, family or corporation—only through some general category." [15] If such a consciousness inhibited the unfolding of certain potentialities of personal uniqueness, the individual was well compensated by the stability and the "given" meaning which the communal context provided for his life. The new social, economic, and cultural forces that stemmed from the Renaissance, and later were greatly intensified by the Enlightenment and the Commercial and Industrial Revolutions, all conspired toward the breaking of these ties. Whether by voluntary action (in the case of the new "heroic" personalities) or by manipulation at the hands of social trends (as in the case of the mass of men), the individual was cast loose from his communal moorings, henceforth to be dependent solely on his own achievements for his sense of personal fulfilment, as well as for his social status and his economic sustenance.

As an ideal pervading much of modern philosophy, both popular and academic, individualism generally meant that each person was to be valued for himself, regardless of his particular gifts or achievements. In the stress of the strongly competitive patterns of modern life itself, however, this creed was gradually

[15] Jakob Burckhardt, *Civilization of the Renaissance in Italy*, trans. S.G.C. Middlemore (London: Phaidon Press, 1950), p. 81.

transmuted into a reverence rather for the *successful* individual. The American milieu provided in the phenomenon of the open frontier—a re-enactment on the national scale of the classic European age of exploration and expansion — an especial re-enforcement for the competitive motif; and here particularly the goal of individual "success" has been the most widespread and the most pervasive.

Thus even the infants in American society seem to be caught up in the mood of competition, for as certain observers have pointed out, the American mother delights in nothing more than in comparing her child's achievements with those of others on the block, or with the par performance levels established by the experts. Likewise, in school, the child is taught to prize the visible marks of success. Among teen-agers and college students, the "rating and dating" system frequently converts even social relationships into counters in the competitive game. The American woman is noted for her facility in the pursuit of a special and subtly-differentiated variety of prestige-giving activities and objects. Meanwhile, her husband is equally caught up in the competitive scheme through his struggle to "get ahead" in the world of work. An important reason for the frequent failure of the modern man—even one with a fairly responsible position—to develop a sense of genuine vocation in his work, is the fact that he regards his job not as an end in itself, but only as a step on the ladder to the next higher level.

That not even the American democratic faith has proved able to counteract these persistent tendencies toward status ranking, is demonstrated in recent studies of American communities. The anthropologist who carried out the study of a small farming town in the southern Midwest reported in *Plainville, U.S.A.* indicates that this particular community was chosen precisely because it was believed to be socially homogeneous, i.e., to lack well-defined social classes. His studies soon forced him to recognize, however, that in actuality the life even of this small community was characterized by "a discrimination system of enormous complexity." In reporting the phrases used by the townsfolk themselves to convey these status differentiations, the anthropologist notes that the particular flavor of the terminology depends on the position of the person using it. To those toward the top of the social scale, those toward the bottom were known as "the lower element"; while to those below, the classes above were "people who *think* they're better." The majority of the citizenry in the middle group referred to themselves simply as "all us good honest average everyday working people who try to live right and to do right"—although some divergence did appear between the churchgoers and the nonreligious elements of this stratum, the latter labeling the former as "all the church hypocrites who try to keep people from making a living and having a good time." [16]

In urban communities where the size and relative impersonality of the social system prohibit the development of so closely knit a scheme of subjective evaluations, the same function is served by more objective status indices. Of these, the neighborhood in which one lives and the make of automobile one drives are perhaps the most universally accepted symbols; but under the continual barrage of prestige appeal in modern advertising, almost any object of utility or enjoyment can assume this role of marking the man or woman of distinction. An economic basis for such stratification is provided by the very real differentials in income still obtaining in America, despite the graduated income tax. Research has demonstrated how not only personal manners and style of life, but patterns of child rearing, educational achievement, and even church membership can be correlated with differing positions in the class and status hierarchy. W. Lloyd Warner reports, for instance, that the "modern" or "progressive" philosophy of child rearing has been far more prevalent among middle-class than among lower-class families; though he adds,

[16] James West (a pseudonym), *Plainville, U.S.A.* (New York: Columbia Univ. Press, 1945), pp. 115 ff.

96

significantly, that many middle-class mothers, while professing the prevailing ideology, in practice also follow more traditional patterns.[17]

The largely open character of the American class system of course distinguishes it from that of an hierarchical society in the traditional sense. It is always possible for the individual, by virtue of his achievements, to rise to a higher level. But likewise, it is always possible for him to fall—if not absolutely, as in times of economic crisis, then relatively (to "fall behind" in the competitive status-struggle); and herein lie deep-seated sources of psychic insecurity. The medieval man felt no anxiety concerning his position, whether it was high or low, since he knew that he was bound to it for life. The modern American can never relax his efforts to maintain a toe hold in the socio-economic order.

Even those who are outwardly able to achieve success as our culture defines it seem to be strangely subject to disillusionment. A familiar figure to the American psychiatrist is the middle-aged individual who already has achieved his competitively-defined objectives, but now has come to doubt the worth of these very achievements. Perhaps even worse than the sense of guilt that may overtake such a man when he reviews the means he has employed, is the sheer sense of emptiness in his present existence, now that a plateau in the life struggle has been reached. The isolation and hostility between man and man produced by such competitiveness, moreover, mean the thwarting of a deep inner need for fellowship.

It is noteworthy that already in the Renaissance, when Western culture first embarked on its emphasis on the self-reliant individual, there were anticipations of the profound psychic perils involved in such a course. Even in the paintings of Michelangelo, who in his own career as well as in his artistic work seemed to embody the most expansive possibilities of the new individualism,

[17] W. Lloyd Warner, *American Life: Dream and Reality* (Chicago: Univ. of Chicago Press, 1953), pp. 98 ff.

there can be discerned the marks of tension and even of despair:

Consciously Michelangelo gloried in the individualistic struggle, defiantly accepting the isolation it involved. . . . But in his paintings can be seen the tension and conflict which were the underlying psychological counterpart of the excessive individualism. His figures on the Sistine chapel exhibit a continuous restlessness and perturbation. . . . Almost all of Michelangelo's human beings, powerful and triumphant as they appear at first glance, present on closer inspection the *dilated eyes which are a tell-tale sign of anxiety*.[18]

A NATION OF NOMADS

"Vertical mobility" is the term frequently used by sociologists to describe the open character of the American class and status system. Equally characteristic of the American people, and perhaps equally contributory to psychic turmoil, is their "horizontal" mobility—i.e., their propensity to move from place to place.

When William Attwood, the perceptive foreign correspondent of *Look* magazine, returned to the United States in 1955 after nine years overseas, he spent three months traveling from coast to coast to get reacquainted with the country. It is significant that in his report, Attwood's first exclamation in describing the changes that he noted was: "Everybody's on the move!"

Does anybody stay put anymore? In Odessa, Texas, we found that sixty-six out of seventy high school kids were born some place else; many had lived in more than four states. In Greenville, Mississippi, we went to a farewell party for a couple moving west; only two of the sixteen present could call it their home town. Everywhere you find veterans who liked it where they were stationed, married local girls and settled down—for a while.

We're becoming a nation of nomads.[19]

[18] Rollo May, *The Meaning of Anxiety* (New York: Ronald Press, 1950), p. 161.

[19] William Attwood, "A New Look at America," *Look*, July 12, 1955. Attwood has expanded his observations into a book, *Still the Most Exciting Country* (New York: Alfred A. Knopf, 1955).

U.S. Census Bureau experts estimate that in a typical year of the early 1950's, more than thirty million Americans changed their place of residence: one in five of the entire population. Of these, twenty million remained within the same county, while ten million moved outside the county; and of the latter, five million moved outside the state—all this within just twelve months.

The consequences of such an unusual sociological development are difficult to estimate; but if one considers merely the effect upon American children of such disruptions of their school programs as well as of their peer group relationships, one can hardly view the situation with equanimity. Likewise for adults, there are bound to be serious psychological consequences from the repeated breaking of ties with friends, neighbors, the local church, and other groups—ties in which the meaningful stuff of human life ordinarily so largely resides.

Alongside this mobility in space, another striking feature of modern culture is what we might term its "mobility in time"—that is, the rapidity of social change, together with the expectation of such change which has become engrained in our character. Again, this widespread motif of Western culture is found at its greatest intensity in the United States.

Visitors from abroad, and particularly from the lands of the Far East, have remarked that Americans seem to be perpetually in a hurry, though they seldom are certain toward what they are hurrying. They do know, however, what they are moving *from:* namely, the past. For the unquestioned presupposition of our attitude and action is that "the new is better." No lasting value is to be attached to the attainments even of the recent past; much less would modern man look toward a heritage from musty antiquity for moral or social wisdom. The manufacturers of American automobiles have been probably the shrewdest in capitalizing on this demand for up-to-dateness, finding even the smallest modifications in style or accouterments sufficient to promote new-model cars each year. Americans in this respect would more than qualify for the description accorded the Athenians in the Book of Acts, the passion of whose lives was "either to tell or hear (or, we would add, to possess) some new thing."

Much as it may be taken for granted by the present generation, such an attitude toward the past is by no means a universal human trait. It is our own epoch, as one critic has remarked, that "has invented the trick of glorying in the fact of its own existence. Modernity's way of priding itself on its modernity is entirely modern." [20] In view of the actual scale and tempo of social change that has been man's experience during the past few centuries, the growth of such an attitude was perhaps inevitable. To acknowledge the inevitability, however, means only to perceive more clearly the tragic character of the development of this insulation in time, which has cut man off from any sense of rootage in a great tradition, and has made unavailable to him the finest resources of the past.

The rapidity of social change and its accompanying attitudes are largely responsible, too, for the problem of the "gulf between the generations" which looms so large especially for teen-age youth and their parents. The specific values and customs cherished by those who have long since settled into their own life patterns are, in fact, frequently out of touch with the situation and the needs of the oncoming generation. The problem is greatly accentuated, however, by the common antipathy toward accepting guidance from those identified with the past. The struggle to avoid such identification no doubt accounts for much of the strong emphasis on youthfulness in our culture, an emphasis which produces the rather pathetic spectacle of men and women well advanced in middle age rejecting their own maturity for the pursuit of a perennial adolescence. Equally distressing is the psychic predicament of the elderly in our society. Far from looking to those of advancing years as the source of wisdom and of leader-

[20] Charles Baudouin, *The Myth of Modernity* (London: George Allen and Unwin, 1950), p. 2.

ship for the community, as has been the case in many societies (including the world of the Old Testament), by compulsory retirement and by our accent on youthfulness we divest the aged of either social or economic function. No matter what advances we may make toward providing for the physical needs of those in the concluding years of life, their need for a genuinely significant role in the community will remain the more serious problem.

In many of these respects, our culture can be understood in terms of a distinction that anthropology has made between "place-minded" and "time-minded" populations. Rural, primitive, or slowly changing cultures, such as those traditionally characteristic of Asia, tend to produce persons who are humble about their own moment in history, but proud of the past and attached to the place in which their life is set. They look down on their neighbors, but look up to their ancestors. An urbanized, progressive culture, in contrast, fosters pride in up-to-dateness, while tradition is disparaged. Conformity to fashion reigns, while deviations according to locality are looked down upon as backward. Such "civilized" societies, A. L. Kroeber comments, resemble "a vast, flat, quivering surface"; the folk societies, "a long, tough, firmly-grasping root." [21] Without doubt, the peoples of the modern West and Americans in particular are of the strongly time-minded type.

So strong, in fact, is our emphasis upon modernity that even the present becomes devalued in favor of the future. One can never be certain that conditions will long remain the same; therefore, it would clearly be unwise to invest their present configuration with much significance. As the saying goes, "I wouldn't want to get involved." The American is proverbial for his ability to adjust quickly to new and strange circumstances; but by the same token, he finds it difficult really to savor his present experiences or to develop depth relationships. Adding to all these tend-

[21] A. L. Kroeber, *Anthropology* (New York: Harcourt, Brace and Co., 1948), pp. 610ff.

encies toward a flavorless and superficial sort of life is, finally, what has been called our "loss of ritual"—the disappearance, in the solvent of secularism combined with atomistic individualism, of "that communal ceremony and celebration, those feasts and fasts, pomps and jubilees, pilgrimages and holy days, which played so large a part in the older world." It was such "focuses of sanctity in time and place," as Amos Wilder has reminded us, that "constantly asserted and communicated the deeper sanctions for existence, and kept alive in man a sense of its mysterious ground." [22]

RELIANCE ON TECHNIQUES

In modern man's triumphant march toward the good society and toward the fulfilment of all human desires, science was to have been his greatest instrument. Once the methods of science had been extended to all realms of life and the blessings of technology shared among all people, the millenium would virtually have arrived.

The collapse of this enchanting vision in our own day was marked at perhaps its most climactic moment by J. Robert Oppenheimer's comment when the first atomic explosion was consummated (after years of work under his own direction) at Alamogordo, New Mexico, in 1945: "In some crude sense which no vulgarity, no overstatement can quite extinguish, the physicists have known sin, and this is a knowledge which they cannot lose." [23] The slow realization of the true horror of Hiroshima and Nagasaki, followed by the almost unbelievable news of the development of weapons of mass destruction whose blasting, killing, maiming power exceeds that of the original atomic bomb by a thousandfold, has brought home even to normally complacent Americans the fact that the scientific dream has indeed turned into a nightmare.

[22] Amos Wilder, *Modern Poetry and the Christian Tradition* (New York: Charles Scribner's Sons, 1952), p. 53.
[23] Quoted in *Time*, April 26, 1954.

To take cognizance of this fact, however, by no means implies that the whole modern scientific enterprise should be condemned as the expression of human pride and sin, as has been the habit of some idealists and medievalists. But it is surely true that the development of scientific technique provides a particularly tempting *occasion* for sin and, when misused, a demonically effective *instrument* of sin. Moreover, as Gabriel Marcel has pointed out, no matter how admirable might be the intellectual discipline, disinterestedness, and creativity of the great scientific thinker or even the typical inventor or research man, the general populace in no way shares in that primary creative experience. They know science only through its results—whether for good or evil.

The results indeed seem increasingly to be evil, or at best ambiguous. Meant to serve as man's greatest instrument for the control of his environment, technology seems rather to have gained the dominance over man. The depersonalizing effects of the predominance of the machine, and of the "rationalization" of industrial procedure, have been noted by many critics. The human being in the typical modern plant is permitted merely to serve as "feeder," "watcher," or at the most "fixer" for the mechanical apparatus. Not so often noted is the equally poignant plight of the office clerk, who is submerged in a sea of filing cards rather than chained to the assembly line. And if the life of the outer office is circumscribed by the routine of typewriter, comptometer, addressograph, and file, even the existence of the junior executive is largely defined by the shuttle between telephone and dictaphone.

On the basis of newspaper headlines during 1955, someone has remarked that we now live in the "age of the IBM" in a double sense—the Intercontinental Ballistics Missile, latest in the series of superweapons, and the familiar office fixture of IBM recording, filing, sorting, calculating, printing, and now even "thinking" machines. Not even farming has been exempt from this seemingly irreversible trend toward mechanization.

The manner in which the whole pace of his life has been speeded up to match the tempo of the machine is probably imperceptible to the average urbanized American, unless he chances to find himself temporarily transferred from his regular habitat to some rural or natural environment. His very body seems to revolt against such unwonted quietude, leaving him restless until he finds his rest again in—the routine. Such might be the underlying cause of the proverbially frantic, mile-chasing character of the American "vacation." How ridiculous now appears the trepidation felt by the generation of fifty or seventy-five years ago at traveling in horseless carriage or railway car at the fabulous speed of twenty or thirty miles an hour! Today, test pilots fly at four-figure speeds faster than the earth's own rotation. So much taken for granted is this pattern of repeated adjustments to ever faster and more complex devices, that it appears to cause little shock when *Life* magazine documents the emergence of "Jet Age Man": "New breed of flier merges with plane like living computing machine." [24]

It is precisely the ineradicable difference between a man and a machine which our culture is in mortal danger of forgetting. Martin Buber has put us all in his debt by his insistence on this point, in terms of his famous distinction between "I-Thou" and "I-It" relationships. There are two ways, says Buber, in which I can relate myself to the world: according to the pattern "I-It," which is a subject-object relation; or according to the pattern of "I-Thou," which implies that I am confronted not by an object but by another subject. Only the latter constitutes a truly human relationship: the recognition of the other as a unique, free, and responsible human being such as myself. Our temptation is to carry over the "I-It" attitude from the material world to the

[24] *Life*, December 6, 1954.

world of persons—a fault to which the scientific and technological mind is particularly prone. The qualities of tentativeness and objectivity are undoubtedly essential in the scientific laboratory, and the technician must almost by definition take an exploitative attitude toward his material. But when transferred to the realm of interpersonal relationships, these same attitudes have withering effects—encouraging detachment rather than commitment, obtuseness instead of sympathy, and, in general, the use of other persons as means toward one's own ends. Whether in the social, economic, or political order, the individual is no longer valued for his uniqueness, but considered merely one of countless interchangeable, and therefore expendable, parts. Even one's wife can be turned in for a new model if her usefulness to one's pleasure or prestige deteriorates.

From this standpoint, the latest achievement of our scientific culture—the perfection of the instruments of mass communication—is seen to embody a pervasive threat to personality. For by its very nature, mass communication, numbering its audiences in the millions and tens of millions, can have no concern for the individual as such; he is merely the anonymous reader, viewer, or consumer who provides a digit in the ever-more-astronomical figures which the magazine, radio, or television network can present to its advertisers. Nor can such mass communication be a two-way, subject to subject relationship: the flow of news, entertainment, propaganda, and cajolery is strictly in a one-way direction, radiating outward from the gigantic nerve centers in New York and Hollywood. Thus it is an exceedingly short step, or none at all, from mass communication to mass manipulation.

In the United States there fortunately has been little effort thus far to capture the media for ideological or political purposes. Rather than aspiring Fuehrers, here it has been the hucksters of branded consumer goods who have become the experts in mass psychology. "Give away" and "tear jerker" programs have followed the lead of the commercials in appealing to every variety of human desire and sentiment. And from here it is only another short step to the cult of "public relations" which has blighted the integrity of so many fine causes and institutions; to the "human engineering" which in management circles has come forward as a more subtle instrument of paternalism; and to the "engineering of consent" in the political domain by pressure group employment of the same techniques.

Though we recognize that there remains a vast difference between what might be called the "soft" and "hard" varieties of mass manipulation, as represented respectively by American advertising and totalitarian propaganda, it is still pertinent for us to heed the testimony of those who have experienced the latter. It was in the neo-primitive Nazi regime that we had perhaps the most frightening example of "mechanized barbarians" in possession of the "barbarous mechanisms" of our time. The French philosopher Gabriel Marcel has spoken of the cruelties inflicted on the inmates of Nazi concentration camps as "techniques of degradation," with the implication that they represent but the ultimate point in the development of manipulative methods. He quotes a Polish woman who, after giving details of the terrible mismanagement of the camp at Auschwitz in which she was interned, states:

And now I understood. I understood that it was not a matter of disorder or lack of organization, but that on the contrary it was a mature and conscious principle which had presided over the installation of the camp. We had been condemned to perish in our own dirt, to drown ourselves in mud, in our own excrements; the point was to abase us, to drag us down to the level of the beasts, to fill us with horror and contempt for ourselves and our fellow-sufferers.[25]

If, says Marcel, our view of man is realistic enough to acknowledge how deep-set in human nature this "wish to degrade" is,

[25] Gabriel Marcel, *Man Against Mass Society* (Chicago: Henry Regnery Co., 1952), p. 31.

the question arises whether it is possible in the long run for the victims of such persecution to avoid being contaminated by the example of their persecutors. Americans had special cause for self-examination in this respect when they learned in late 1955 of the establishment by their own Air Force of a "school of torture" devoted to the dress rehearsal of the "brain washing" methods first employed against Americans by the Chinese Communists. Many questioned whether the degradation thus experienced by tortured and torturers alike did not more than cancel out the presumed advantage of "teaching them what to expect." Ambiguous indeed are the fruits of modern man's devotion to the perfection of techniques.

THE MASS MAN OF TODAY

In summary, the modern man has suffered a severe depersonalization and alienation from the sources of meaningful existence. He has been an extremely lonely individual, experiencing a perhaps unprecedented combination of cosmic and social homelessness. For some, this loneliness has proved to be, in the final analysis, creative rather than destructive. Removal of all the accustomed securities has spurred them toward a deeper self-awareness, and prevented their relying on any but the ultimate resource. But for the majority, the anxieties of modern life have only served to drive them to seek refuge in new collectivities— a trend most spectacularly evidenced by the totalitarian mass movements of our century.

We seem, in fact, to be witnessing at the present time a change in the character structure of the typical man so great as to mark probably the end of one whole era in Western history and the beginning of another. Just as in the economic order the individualism of the past few centuries now has issued in a private or state collectivism, so in the realm of personality the typically self-sufficient individual is being replaced by a new collectivistic man. If the former be designated as the "modern" man, the latter must be termed the man of the "post-modern" period.

This is the historic change which David Riesman is recording when he speaks of the increasingly "other-directed" character of the contemporary American. The typical man of the modern period in Western culture was, in Riesman's terms, a strongly "inner-directed" individual. Having shaken loose the bonds of the tradition-directed medieval society, he struck out on his own course of life, guided as if by an inner gyroscope toward his individually determined goals—goals, however, which remained within the bounds of a rather fixed moral framework. The man of humanistic culture and the Puritan believer were equally examples of this inner-directed type. Neither of them, of course, has wholly disappeared from our society; nor have the last representatives of the tradition-directed man. The dominant tendency of our day, however, is of another sort; the individual now tends to look for guidance as to right and wrong not to a distinctive cultural inheritance, or to a Divine Command, but to the opinions of his contemporaries. The thoughts and feelings of the "others," changeable as they may be, are his guide to manners, morals, and an accepted style of life. It is as if the gyroscope holding the individual on a predetermined course had been replaced with radar antennae enabling him continually to veer and tack in accordance with the psychological environment.[26]

Among the factors making for this change, Riesman has emphasized the importance of the "democratic" pattern of family relationships to which we have referred. The parents' abdication of (or eviction from) their authoritative role has left the child no source of guidance except his contemporaries. The smaller size of the family has forced the child to find companionship

[26] David Riesman with Nathan Glazer and Reuel Denney, *The Lonely Crowd: A Study in the Changing American Character* (New Haven: Yale Univ. Press. 1950). Cf. Riesman's *Individualism Reconsidered and Other Essays* (Glencoe, Ill.: Free Press, 1954).

among his age-mates. And his parents' continual parental stress on the need to "learn to get along" with the peer group has reinforced the tendency. Meanwhile the public schools seem largely to have fallen prey to a similar philosophy. The promotion of "good adjustment" by the eradication of personal quirks that might interfere with smooth integration into the group has become so predominant a goal among some educationalists that not only has individual uniqueness been discouraged, but the content of the curriculum itself often has been emasculated. It is small wonder then that among American teen-agers the highest value comes to be that of perfect conformity to the fashions of the crowd.

In the world of business, other-directedness is fostered for its commercial value. The shop girl is instructed that "the customer is always right"; the salesman is advised that he must "sell himself" if he would sell his goods. "In many strata of white collar employment," C. Wright Mills observes, "such traits as courtesy, helpfulness, and kindness, once intimate, are now part of the impersonal means of livelihood." [27] It is this experience of oneself as a salable commodity that produces among contemporary Americans an outlook that Erich Fromm has called the "marketing orientation":

This feeling might be compared to that of a commodity, of handbags on a counter, for instance, could they feel and think. Each handbag would try to make itself as "attractive" as possible in order to attract customers and to look as expensive as possible in order to obtain a higher price than its rivals. The handbag sold for the highest price would feel elated, since that would mean it was the most "valuable" one; the one which was not sold would feel sad and convinced of its own worthlessness. This fate might befall a bag which, though excellent in appearance and usefulness, had the bad luck to be out of date because of a change in fashion.

[27] C. Wright Mills, *White Collar: The American Middle Classes* (New York: Oxford Univ. Press, 1951), p. xvii.

Like the handbag, one has to be in fashion on the personality market, and in order to be in fashion one has to know what kind of personality is most in demand.[28]

How does one learn what is the latest model for personality? To some extent through formal education channels; but far more powerfully, in present-day America, such models are conveyed by the mass media—television, movies, and magazines, including advertising. The most direct source, of course, is the individual's own "radar" sensitivity to the changing expectations of his associates.

William H. Whyte, Jr., in one of his memorable studies of the mind of the typical corporation executive, has noted amusedly how the so-called science of "human engineering" now being avidly pursued by personnel men and industrial relations managers, has invented a new terminology to justify conformism.

Now one no longer need be ashamed of going along with the herd; indeed, with the aid of the new jargon he can be articulately proud of the fact. He is not just conforming, he is using "group skills." He is maintaining "equilibrium." He is "participating." [29]

Not only is the young college graduate now entering the business world more concerned for security in the established system than for pioneering opportunities, but even his wife, as Whyte discovered, is subject to molding into a corporation model. The smallest instance of personal peculiarity or social nonconformity on her part may permanently ruin her husband's chances for advancement.[30]

[28] Erich Fromm, *Man for Himself: An Inquiry into the Psychology of Ethics* (New York: Rinehart & Co., 1947), pp. 70 ff.

[29] William H. Whyte, Jr., with the editors of *Fortune, Is Anybody Listening?: How and Why U.S. Business Fumbles When It Talks with Human Beings* (New York: Simon and Shuster, 1952), p. xi.

[30] *Ibid.*, pp. 148ff. In his more recent volume, *The Organization Man* (New York: Simon and Schuster, 1956), Whyte has broadened and further documented his indictment of managerial conformism.

With such trends in evidence throughout our society, it is hardly surprising that the prophets of super-Americanism should have found such a fertile field during the decade following the Second World War. By the mid-fifties, it was possible to discern that the majority of Americans had never been so exercised over the threat of Communism as the headlines had implied; yet the number of them prepared to deny the right to teach, to speak, or even to work, not only to Communists but to other "non-conformists," remained alarmingly high. Moreover, the legal tradition of "due process" designed to safeguard those rights already had been seriously damaged, if not permanently undermined.[31]

More than a hundred years ago, Alexis de Tocqueville issued a warning in his classic study *Democracy in America* that seems remarkably pertinent today. Only in this nation, he observed, had the principle of equality then newly abroad in the world attained genuine embodiment in the concrete circumstances of life. Here, in truth, there existed neither aristocracy nor princely tyranny. Yet, asked de Tocqueville, did not this unprecedented "equality of conditions" itself pose a fateful threat—that of the "tyranny of the majority"? In the processes of government, de Tocqueville warned, rule of the majority could mean dominance of erratic public moods rather than reasoned leadership. In the realm of character and attitude formation, he foresaw precisely the sort of conformism of which we have been speaking.

The nearer people are drawn to the common level of an equal and similar condition, the less prone does each man become to place implicit faith in a certain man of a certain class of men. But his readiness to believe the multitude increases, and opinion is more than ever mistress of the world. . . . In the principle of equality I very

[31] On the latter point, see Adam Yarmolinsky, *Case Studies in Personnel Security* (Bureau of National Affairs, 1955). On the state of popular opinion, cf. Samuel Stouffer, *Communism, Conformity, and Civil Liberties: A Cross-Section of the Nation Speaks Its Mind* (New York: Doubleday and Co., 1955).

clearly discern two tendencies; one leading the mind of every man to untried thoughts, the other prohibiting him from thinking at all. . . . [32]

Like de Tocqueville's, our estimate of the principle of equality must be ambivalent. As a demand for the removal of injustice, this principle has been the glory of American democracy, responsible in large measure for continued action to ameliorate the lot of the poor, the rise of labor to a status of dignity and self-determination, and the continuing struggle against racial discrimination. But when it becomes interpreted in terms of an erasure not merely of injustice but of all differentia among individuals, then "equality" becomes a debilitating principle. The notion that men and women should be not only equal but alike, or that it is undemocratic to provide special opportunities for gifted youth, or that the American "melting pot" means that the rich cultural inheritance of immigrant groups must be sloughed off in favor of the pallid image of the "typical" American—such might be listed as some of the unfortunate effects of this interpretation. Of similar import is the question raised recently by a group concerned over the mediocre state of much of our literature, art, and entertainment: "Can we have an Age of the Common Man without making it an Age of the Common Denominator?" [33]

But we should have to add to de Tocqueville's analysis, from the perspective of our own century, that the "equality of conditions" in itself would never have been sufficient to account for the intensity of the new collectivism in character as well as culture that is manifest today. The Age of Conformity is a direct precipitate of the Age of Anxiety, of the whole psychic malaise of the contemporary world. Eric Hoffer, that shrewd lay philosopher who wrote a masterpiece of social psychology while plying

[32] Alexis de Tocqueville, *Democracy in America,* ed. Phillips Bradley (New York: Vintage Books, 1954), II, 11 ff.

[33] Joseph Wood Krutch *et al., Is the Common Man Too Common?* (Norman: Univ. of Oklahoma Press, 1954).

his trade as longshoreman up and down the American coasts, supports such an analysis when he asserts that it is in "people who see their lives as irremediably spoiled" that mass movements find their membership. A mass movement, Hoffer concludes, owes its fervent following primarily to "the refuge it offers from the anxieties, barrenness, and meaninglessness of an individual existence." [34] This holds true not only of the explicitly totalitarian regimes, but also (though admittedly with less intensity) of the conformist tendencies in our own society. Indeed, in Hoffer's view it holds true also of the church, which is likewise a mass movement providing merely a religious variation on the fundamental theme.

The question posed by the contemporary man, if not articulately then implicitly, is whether there is not a decisive difference in the alternative offered by the church. His experience with the secular collectivisms soon reveals that they are based not on fulfilment but on atrophy of personal existence. His question then is whether in the Christian faith he can find a ground for genuine community that will not crush but foster meaningful individuality, while offering a source of courage adequate even to the travail of this anxious age.

BIBLIOGRAPHY

Among readily available paper-bound books pertinent to this chapter are David Riesman's *The Lonely Crowd* (New York: Anchor Books, 1953), C. G. Jung's *Modern Man in Search of a Soul* (New York: Harvest Books, 1955), José Ortega y Gasset's *The Revolt of the Masses* (New York: Mentor Books, 1950), and Alexis de Tocqueville's *Democracy in America* (2 vols.; New York: Vintage Books, 1954).

C. Wright Mills' *White Collar* (New York: Oxford Univ. Press, 1951) will be found one of the most fascinating of recent social-psychological studies. For an interpretative survey of modern fiction,

[34] Eric Hoffer, *The True Believer: Thoughts on the Nature of Mass Movements* (New York: Harper & Bros., 1951).

poetry, and drama, see *Spiritual Problems in Contemporary Literature*, edited by Stanley Romaine Hopper (New York: Harper & Bros., 1952). Many of the writings of Paul Tillich are of direct relevance, especially *The Courage to Be* (New Haven: Yale Univ. Press, 1952) and chapters in *The Protestant Era* (Chicago: Univ. of Chicago Press, 1948), as well as his sermons. Wayne Oates' *Anxiety in Christian Experience* (Philadelphia: Westminster Press, 1955) is brief but comprehensive, biblically grounded, and closely oriented to the work of the pastor.

CHAPTER 4

False Hopes and the Gospel

by Martin J. Heinecken

THE HUMAN SITUATION IN OUR DAY

Evidence that something has gone wrong with our boasted civilization is written large over the face of the globe. There have been many diagnoses and many proffered panaceas. Many a delegation is sent from the once fiery prophets of reform, now languishing in the dungeon of their doubts: "Art thou he that should come, or look we for another?" What is the answer? Is there a decisive "either-or"? Can the gospel be distinguished from the false hopes?

There is growing conviction that the dissolution of the forms of community in our day is caused by severance from the living God and by the increasing autonomy of a culture not undergirded by the decisive biblical-Christian categories. The struggle today is the struggle between individualism and collectivism. On the one hand is an extreme individualism in which each one goes his own way, striving to fulfil himself by charting his own course and using others only as it suits him. On the other hand, there is collectivism in which the individual counts for nothing. The individual is lost in the masses; he is regimented in thought and actions; he is a tool of the tyrants of the state. At the bottom of both extremes lies the failure to understand what it means to be an individual before the living God.

The peculiar developments aggravating this situation have been delineated in the previous chapters. But it is crucial to note that even before the full effects of these developments were apparent, before workers as well as managers became cogs in a colossus, the "mass man" and the loss of both individuality and community were anticipated.[1] The loss was attributed to lack of realization of what it means to be a man in the Christian sense: a strictly isolated center of responsibility, called to decision at every moment and held eternally responsible for that decision, yet unable to be a true individual except in community, except as he really receives his life, here and hereafter, as the gift of love from his Creator and Redeemer.

The leveling process which reduces everyone to the lowest common denominator was noted. It was recognized that if there is to be true community there must first of all be true individuals. This was seen to be impossible if all the decisive distinctions are blurred, first of all the absolute qualitative difference between God and man, and then the decisive differences between man and man, the distinction between male and female, between ruler and ruled, between true greatness and mediocrity, and all those individual differences that result from each individual's actual station in life. Where these distinctions are not recognized, people band together in groups and try to find strength in numbers while each one is afraid ever to be alone.

It has been shown that many of the elements of the social structure which gave man a measure of security and significance have been destroyed. The capitalist system, industrialization, urbanization, the scientific method, etc., have all played their part. The structures that once gave a measure of stability and meaning to life have lost much of their cohesive power. In this loss, the precariousness of the human situation at all times has been immeasurably aggravated. Living without a transcendent refuge in the world, men have been robbed even of the partial refuge which

[1] Cf. S. Kierkegaard, *The Present Age* (New York: Oxford Univ. Press, 1940).

a meaningful this-worldly existence might afford. Hence, they are on the lookout for saviors and are easy prey for the false hopes that claim to give them the status and the security they lack.

If there is to be a defense against such false hopes, there must be a realistic appraisal of what it means to exist, not just in the twentieth century, but in any century, as a human being who literally stands out (ex-ist) from the flux of time while nevertheless being involved in it, and who is a synthesis of necessity and freedom, of eternity and time.

To begin with, there is always the givenness of the human situation over which man has no control whatsoever. He finds himself spewn into existence. There is the accident of birth, of heredity, and of environment, coupled with the determinisms of nature. A man does not choose his father and mother. The time and place of a man's birth are an inexorable destiny. The genes of heredity indicate the most rigid kind of determinism, the picture imprinted on the undeveloped negative of a man's capacities is fixed, and factors beyond his control determine the process of the development of that negative from the moment the sperm hits the ovum in the precarious shelter of the womb.

The story of the determinism of nature is well enough known, though not always seriously enough appraised. Much has been made of late of Heisenberg's principle of indeterminacy which makes prediction impossible at a certain level of atomic behavior. But it is obvious that such indeterminacy has no effect whatsoever on the inviolable chain of cause and effect and the methods and the success of the scientist. He can go right on making H-bombs and be convinced that when the bombs are dropped there is every probability that the explosion will occur. We are not beyond the unutterable awe with which Kant faced the starry skies above; that is, the inviolable order of nature—and we are no nearer a solution of how, in such a world, to salvage our freedom.

Above all, the givenness of existence must be taken out of the realm of abstract discussion. The givenness of existence is a matter of actual experience in a concrete situation when a specific individual finds himself confronted with the full accident of his birth and, let us say, the fact that his one child is crippled with cerebral palsy, his other child has leukemia, and he himself is out of a job in one of those recurring depressions that can be so neatly graphed by the expert economist. In other chapters there is abundant illustration of the way in which men are the helpless victims of their environment.

To this we must add the unpredictable turns of fate, which the most careful planning cannot evade. The Greek tragedians knew whereof they spoke. Oedipus, ignorant of his parentage, in his very efforts to avoid his destiny, slays his father and marries his mother. In *The Wall*, Jean Paul Sartre describes an apprehended member of the resistance movement as he faces death. He is determined to be master of the situation and not to betray his comrades. Outwardly he remains calm, but suddenly he notices that, like a child, he has been unable to control himself. There is a physical compulsion that overcomes him unawares. Then, in an effort to save his comrades, he reveals to his captors the most unlikely place he can think of as his comrades' hiding place, and that is exactly where they are found, for they, too, had chosen the most unlikely place. Everyone can multiply from his own experience such meaningless turns of fate which upset the most carefully laid plans and pulverize the most adamant decisions.

Then there is always the one absolute certainty of death. It still remains true, as the Greek sage said, that nature means to kill us all and will eventually succeed. The moment we are born we are old enough to die, and all life from that moment on is nothing but dying. The artery has already been cut, and each pulse beat sends the blood spurting to seep into the sands from which it can never be gathered up again. Before this one inevitable certainty, man must feel his absolute helplessness, and no one can resign himself to that with equanimity. If death ends all, how absolutely meaningless all our fitful strivings then become!

Death is like a sopping sponge rubbed over the ebony slate of life, erasing every trace of meaning written there, leaving nothing but blackness. A sentence can have no meaning when it breaks off in the middle.

So all-encompassing are these determinacies that it seems impossible to salvage even the slightest sliver of freedom. Yet this is the mystery of life, this absolute paradox, which man has not yet succeeded in resolving: though "absolutely" determined, yet man is "absolutely" free and responsible. It would be the most fanatic devotion to a creed to deny this freedom. It is like Zeno denying the fact of motion because it confounded his intellect. If a man were no more free than the stone hurled through the air, it would not be possible for him to speak of responsibility, obligation, justice, integrity, and whatever other words make up his moral vocabulary. As stated elsewhere, it is an axiom of the scientific method to be determined by the facts and not by some speculative theory. We must count the teeth in the horse's mouth and not deduce their number from a universal and necessary (a priori) principle. If you are to have it straight from the horse's mouth, surely this fact of freedom is undeniable.

What a maddening, frightening, anguished situation this is! It is no wonder that the specter of meaninglessness looms large and flaps its ghostly wings and gives man the weird goose pimples of nameless dread before nothingness. This is the fearful dread that we find hovering over all existence and which precedes both creativity and sin.

This is man's predicament: He is on the one hand a part of nature and its chain of determinacies; on the other hand he stands outside of that chain in the transcendence of his freedom. With the mystery of his will he can break into the chain and control his destiny, as it would appear to him, absolutely. But then again, he is absolutely frustrated. There are the determinacies of nature, there are the competing wills of others, there is fate, there is death, and over all is the threat of meaninglessness.

How shall man be delivered from this predicament? He is not safely guided by instincts and unwittingly carried along in a determined process. He is called upon to guide his own destiny and yet he is unable to do so. Either he must give up in despair or else he must rise up in frantic defiance against his lot, and this defiance will be only another variant of his despair.

This human predicament is described as "the sickness unto death." [2] It is the despair which holds all men in its grip and for which there is no cure except in faith in the living God who is Lord of all creation. It involves the mystery of selfhood. A self is that center which is able to relate itself to itself. The self, so to speak, jumps out of its skin and dances around in its bones. The self is aware of itself; it looks at itself like an eye that looks out and then looks back at itself. The self judges itself, laughs or frowns at itself, approves or condemns itself. Such a self is either derived or independent. Such a self must either have put itself into this relation so that it can maintain itself in it, control itself, master itself, sustain itself out of itself, be the sole judge of its own actions—or else such a self has been put into this relation to itself by another. In that case it is a derived, dependent self, which is under the scrutiny and the judgment of that other. It not only judges itself, but is being judged. Such a derived, dependent self can never realize itself except as it comes to rest in the being on which it depends. The unwillingness to do this is despair, and every man is in this state of despair, whether he realizes it or not. The fact that a person is not aware of his illness is no guarantee that he is in good health. It takes a physician to make the diagnosis objectively. So it is with many people who live without any conscious knowledge of their despair. They do not really know what it means to be a self. So they live pretty much like the animals from day to day and hand to mouth and not at all like the responsible creatures they are before the living

[2] See S. Kierkegaard, *The Sickness Unto Death* (Princeton: Princeton Univ. Press, 1941).

God. Yet such people are, at bottom, in despair. They cannot live just like animals, simply because they are not animals. Depth psychology reveals how much weird behavior is accounted for by what is active in the subconscious.

Then there is the despair of weakness, which is the despair at the limitations of existence. It is despair at not willing to be oneself, the limited, dependent, sinful self. It is really a problem of self-acceptance and the one who despairs in weakness despairs of the kind of person he is and the way life treats him. It is like just giving up, because you cannot be what you would like to be or have what you would like to have. The limitations of finite and sinful existence are too overpowering. Before God this is sin; it is a wilful refusal to take one's life from God in trust and to have faith that for him all things are possible, even when humanly speaking there is no possibility. It is succumbing to the anxiety for the morrow; it is despairing of the power of God's omnipotent love.

The opposite of this is the despair of defiance. It is despair at willing to be one's self, that is, the kind of self one wants to be in defiance of all circumstance. It, too, involves the problem of self-acceptance. A man will not accept himself as he is, but means to construct himself to suit himself, to create himself, to make himself the kind of self he wills to be, to be the captain of his soul and overcome all the limitations of his finitude, the accusations of his conscience, and the anxieties for the morrow— in short, he means to be autonomous, to be a law unto himself, and to be his own god. So a man grasps for power, he multiplies his possessions, he increases his knowledge, he strains after good-ness. In the eyes of the world, he may be a tremendous success —while fundamentally he is in deep despair.

From the Christian point of view, what makes all these forms of despair sin is that they are *before God*.[3] It is the wilful refusal

[3] *Ibid*, p. 137.

to acknowledge God's presence, to be humbled by him, and to be strengthened by him. It is being offended, being caused to stumble, instead of surrendering in humility and faith. Sin, therefore, is not the breaking of this or that commandment, but it is the orientation of the whole person in the God-relationship. The opposite of sin is not virtue, but faith. Sin is not ignorance, while knowledge is the cure; but sin is an act of will and the cure is the "good news" of God's approach to man in Christ, which is able to take captive that will and thus set it free. Any proffered panacea which is, therefore, not the proclamation of this "good news" is a false gospel, for it is not news and it is not good.

All this may be expressed in a different way. In a profound sense, man is constituted by his relations. He is not a self-subsistent entity, standing on his own base. God alone is that. God alone can *be* in majestic isolation and needs nothing to complete his being. He has no needs which are not satisfied within his own being. In every way he constitutes himself and is not constituted by his relationships. Everything else, however, is constituted by its relationships. There is nothing which is stable and which persists regardless of its relationships; it remains what it is only as long as the relationships remain constant and, inasmuch as these relationships are not constant, it is not constant but is rather in constant flux.

Water, for example, is a liquid at one temperature, at another it is ice, at another it is steam. In one relationship it is a pure fountain welling from the earth, quenching the thirst of man; in another it is a seething, scalding cauldron no life can withstand; or it is a raging torrent of destruction sweeping all before it. Likewise, the sun from which we derive our energy and which seems so constant in its shining is the sun only as long as the rest of the solar system and the other multitudinous systems of suns and stars remain in equilibrium. Change these relationships and the sun that is our life would be our death.

What has happened to the atom, once thought to be stable? There are no stable atoms—no hard, little indivisible pellets of matter of which the world is built like so many bricks. When the atom was split, mankind entered into the new atomic age. So it is also with man. Like the atom, man's soul is unstable and splittable and, therefore, comes into being or goes out of being.

If the soul were an eternal, timeless essence, it would depend on no one; it would be its own god; it could maintain its being out of itself. But no part of man is God; man depends for his being in his entirety upon God; he is constituted by his relationship to God. God has brought him into being "out of nothing"; he depends for his being upon God, and the kind of being he is depends upon the kind of relationship in which he stands to God.

God could push man around into whatever relationship he desired and so make of him whatever he pleased. But man is not a mere puppet. In freedom, by rebelling and cutting himself loose, he can alter the relationship to the God upon whom he depends. But he cannot make the relationship right; he can only submit to the God upon whom he inevitably depends.

This is the one sense of the image of God in which man was created. To be sure, man has powers and prerogatives which set him off from the rest of creation and make him a sort of god or ruler over that creation, able to make it serve his purposes. There may be said to be a "formal" image there, so that man in the "form" of his being reflects the personality of God, as a thinking, feeling, willing being, a center of responsibility. But all this stress on the "formal" image of God is not to lead to supposing that there is a part of man which is itself divine and, therefore, could dispense with God. The image of God refers rather to the reflection in man of the qualities of God when he is in the right relationship to God. The metaphor of the mirror must be taken seriously. An image can be reflected only if a man is standing in front of the mirror, and so a man can reflect the image of God only if he is in the right relationship to that God. Since he is free, he can tear himself loose from that relation and turn his back upon the mirror, so that he does not reflect the image of God. Even when God seeks him out and comes to him, he can turn from him. "This man seeketh sinners and eateth with them," but they spurn his company.

This is the crux of the matter. The true nature of God revealed in Christ is selfless love for the sake of the beloved, which is the only basis of true community. God is the only one who can love unselfishly; he can love the lilies of the field for themselves alone and not just for the sake of their fine-spun garments; he can love man for himself alone and not because he stands plumed in his virtues; he can love man in his unworthiness, his sin, and his rebellion. This is the basis for all true community, for it is only where individuals serve one another unselfishly, each one with the gifts peculiar to him, that there can be true community. Only then do persons remain persons and are not merely things or tools to be used by another for selfish satisfaction. Only then are there true individuals riveted fast to themselves forever by Him who calls each of them by name.

If there is to be true community, the relationship which constitutes man must be this right relationship of love. The temperature in which he lives must be the warmth of love and not the frigid life-destroying blast of seeking for self-realization.

Man reflects the true image of God only when he is in the right God-relationship. The God-relationship, is however, inseparable from the neighbor relationship. It is only in the distinction of the "I" from the "Thou" that a person recognizes himself as a center of responsibility. It is only as a man is confronted with his neighbor who is dependent upon him and upon whom he himself is in turn dependent, that a man can say "I."

> For the ego is a dream
> Till a neighbor's need by name create it.[4]

[4] W. H. Auden, *The Age of Anxiety* (New York: Random House, 1947), p. 8.

When the neighbor's need calls to man to show love, he then becomes aware of himself. This is his responsibility: to love. This is what it means to be a man: to love. This is what it means to be a brother and a neighbor: to love. Only he who had mercy on him was neighbor to the man who fell among the thieves. Only he is in the image of God and is a true human being who reflects in his life the selfless love of the true good Samaritan who reached out to all men in their need without one iota of concern for himself or of ulterior motivation of any kind, but rather was filled with concern only for those who were in need.

Here we have the pattern of true community: life-together-in-love. This is the right climate and the right soil in which men can grow and true community can develop. But where this atmosphere is polluted, men die. Personality and the forms of community disintegrate. The wells of life are poisoned. Man, cut loose from the living God, destroys himself and others. He is power run amuck, a live wire cavorting crazily about because it is cut loose from its purpose. How tremendously important is that individual center of responsibility! A delicate little hand with scarce the power to crush a flea can control all the explosive power of the atom bomb and set in motion a chain reaction to destroy a world. There are these centers of responsibility everywhere—in cars on the highways, in airplanes in the sky, in the marriage bed, in the schoolroom, at the council table, on the rostrum, at the mass meeting, before the microphone—all of them with surges of potential power for good or evil. What they will do depends on how they are constituted by their relationships.

"The gospel" is the good news of God's coming into the right relationship of love with men in Jesus, the Christ. This revelation in Christ then also makes known that the law of all God's creation is "love." Here it is revealed to the eyes of faith that behind the "masks" of his creation stands the God of love, who has so ordered the world that community is actually possible and actively furthered. The state, the economic order, and monogamous marriage are orders of creation. These are not, after the pattern of the Enlightenment, human contracts into which basically self-sufficient Robinson Crusoes enter for additional benefits. These are the structures of life in which all men inevitably are—male or female, ruler or ruled, producer or consumer, manager or laborer—all depending on gifts and talents provided by God to contribute to the life of the whole. Salvation and community are not something which can be arbitrarily achieved; but they can only be received as gifts by accepting that which God has provided: the law of creation, which is love. Love establishes the right relationship and where this is right the whole creation is revealed as the soil and the climate in which love can flourish. But this is not an impersonal law of nature which governs things mechanically. This is a relationship between people who are free to flout the law of God and to end up in despair.

THE NIHILIST'S ANSWER

There are many proposed panaceas to man's plight. Even where one finds the most realistic appraisal of the human situation in a world in which God is dead, all hope is not abandoned. Even the nihilists are not abandoned to their nihilism. Although life for them has no final meaning and there are no absolute values, because there is no God in heaven, man must forge his future by his own will in defiance of the meaninglessness in which all will finally end. This is the extreme of the despair of defiance which means to face and accept its despair honestly. This is the logical end of the road toward which thought travels once it is severed from the living God. Once it is taken seriously that God is dead, there can then be no order or purpose or absolutes of any kind subsisting in a vacuum. All the atheistic existentialists find this a very distressing fact. The only place in the universe where there is any planning or conscious direction is in the mind of man. The universe is wide open and whatever direction any single life will take or what will be the destiny of mankind depends upon the decisions man makes within the inexorable determinacies of the given.

Since he believes there is no God planning or directing the universe, for Jean Paul Sartre, the French atheist, man just "appears," he just "turns up" in existence, for no ultimate reason or purpose, and he "only afterwards defines himself." Man, therefore, is undefinable; he has no nature; he is at first nothing and only afterwards he gets to be something, i.e., whatever he wills himself to be. "There is no human nature, since there is no God to conceive it. . . . Man is nothing else but what he makes himself." [5] The thesis is that "existence precedes essence." Sartre uses the example of a man making a paper cutter. He has the idea in his mind first and then brings it into existence. Here essence, i.e., the idea, precedes existence and the paper cutter, so to speak, expresses this essence. But let us suppose that there is no God and then raise the question about man's essence. Now there is no idea, no essence of which man in his existence is the expression. Man, therefore, has no definable nature which he is in process of realizing. There is no essence of man. Man is whatever he makes himself into. The same is true also of all so-called values and principles of conduct. There is no realm of eternal essences existing either in their own right or in the mind of God to which man's conduct must conform. Absolutes of beauty, truth, and goodness are a chimera. You have only what certain people hold to be beautiful or true or good. In the final analysis each single individual sets up his own truth, his own beauty, his own goodness, his own meaning.

While this would seem to abandon man to chaos, nevertheless Sartre does attempt to be a humanist and to proclaim a gospel which will lead humanity into a better future. If man is what

[5] Jean Paul Sartre, *Existentialism* (New York: Philosophical Library, 1947), p. 18.

he makes himself, this puts the full responsibility for what he is and does on him and he can never beg any excuse.

Existentialism's first move is to make every man aware of what he is and to make the full responsibility for his existence rest on him. And when we say that man is responsible for himself, we do not mean only that he is responsible for his own individuality, but that he is responsible for all men.[6]

In this way Sartre tries to get a humanism out of his extreme individualism. A man is responsible for all men in that what he chooses is always a choice for all men. Since there are no objective standards and everyone makes his own, then each one must consider what happens to others in virtue of his choice. If I choose monogamy, I choose it for everyone, for if I choose monogamy, then I forbid everyone else to touch my wife; I make it imperative that my wife should be faithful to me. So I have chosen monogamy not only for myself, but for everyone. Whatever I choose, I impose the same choice upon all. If I choose communism, then I forbid the private ownership of the means of production and so choose communism for all.

If this is so, then man's life is beset with anguish: he *is* anguish as he feels his total and deep responsibility for the choices he makes. This is the terror of man's freedom and the basis of his humanism. Whatever he chooses, he chooses it for all and there is no one to reassure him that he has made the right choice.

Every man ought to say to himself, "Am I really the kind of man who has the right to act in such a way that humanity might guide itself by my actions?" And if he does not say that to himself, he is masking his anguish.[7]

Furthermore, to add to the terror and anguish, there is the realization that there is no evading a choice; every procrastina-

[6] *Ibid*, p. 19.
[7] *Ibid*, p. 24.

tion, too, is a choice. Each moment, therefore, is a moment of crisis, and is fraught with the terror of full responsibility. Finally, if God does not exist, then we have to face all the consequences of our freedom and our choices alone. There is no God to forgive, no hereafter to make recompense, every man is condemned in his freedom and his complete responsibility. Let him who is heroic choose this humanist path and avoid the pitfall of complete decadence! Most of Sartre's characters are weaklings who do not have the strength to exercise their freedom but surrender to the inevitableness and meaninglessness of the given. While presenting characters who are the best examples of the despair of weakness, characters who just surrender to the harsh realities of existence, at the same time Sartre unwittingly advocates the despair of defiance.

While this view may not seem a live option today, there are many who have become its enthusiastic adherents. It is mentioned here because it is believed to be the only consistent humanist position and illustrates what happens when the attempt is made to salvage human values apart from faith in the living God. To this nihilism, the gospel is the only answer.

THE CHRISTIANITY OF MAIN STREET

To the resolute despair of nihilism, the average modern man's Christianity is scarcely an answer. The Christianity of the average American today is one of moral ideals, a golden rule Christianity.[8] It follows Matthew Arnold's definition of religion as "morality touched with emotion." The "good news" is essentially that the tyrant God of wrath of the Old Testament, who lorded it arbitrarily over men and played gross favorites with certain people because he liked the shape of their noses and the smell of their sacrifices, has been replaced by a God of love. The "good news" is that all men are brothers, and that if they will live in

[8] See Theodore Wedel, *The Christianity of Main Street* (New York: Macmillan Co., 1950).

accordance with the principles of the Sermon on the Mount and do unto others as they would have men do unto them, a world of peace and brotherhood will result.

In this golden rule Christianity, men are not inherently bad, but basically good. They have all kinds of drives, which pull them in various directions: the drive for self-preservation, the pulls of hunger and of sex, the desire to be somebody and to be accepted by the group, etc. There is also human sympathy, a natural suffering with the pain of others, and there is an altruistic drive, which makes a man willing enough to take his neighbor into account, provided he can see the reason. Just enlighten a man's self-interest sufficiently and you can get him to co-operate for the mutual good. The trouble is that people are shortsighted and ignorant and so they cut off their nose to spite their face. They strike back, they hold on to the little they have, they live only for themselves. But the "good news" is that if they will only learn to turn the other cheek, to go the second mile, to lose themselves in the service of others, then life will be rich and full and the kingdom of God will come upon the earth. Jesus is the Master who has set the example of this kind of a life, the rich and abundant life which he came to give all men. Though he died on the cross, he nevertheless had inner satisfactions which compensated him for what he missed. So we must follow his example. The life of service brings its *inner* rewards. We must not get bogged down in a mad scramble for money and material satisfactions, but we must keep before us the high ideals of service and brotherhood and a world of peace and plenty for all (notice the contradiction!), and we must contribute our share. Then we will earn our reward. We need not even ask about any future life, for the satisfactions of such a life of service will be enough in themselves.

The average modern Christian believes that the "good news" is how God will bless us, if only we will "go his way" and even then, when we fail, he takes into account our weakness and he forgives. In addition to the moral values there are, therefore, the religious values. We can have wonderful experiences midst the beauties of nature or in a stately cathedral. There is uplift in music and art and stained glass windows, and in a colorful High Mass. It doesn't, of course, make too much difference whether you are Protestant, Catholic, or Jewish, or, for that matter, Hindu or Mohammedan. They are all different ways to the same goal. Basically they follow the same moral code and the religious uplift is the same. In fact, some non-Christians take the Christian gospel much more seriously than Christians do themselves. There is much greater peace to be found in Oriental mysticism than in most of bustling western Christianity. So we ought also to learn a lesson from their book. Probably the religion of the future will succeed in incorporating the best insights of them all. Christian missionaries, therefore, should not impose their views on others but should rather sit at a round table and pool their views for the good of all. Confucius, Lao-tse, Asoka, Socrates, Plato, Aristotle, and then finally Jesus! These are the great leaders of mankind. From the Greeks comes our love of beauty, from the Romans our sense of justice, and from Jesus the ideal of an all-embracing love and universal brotherhood. We have never given these "a real try," but if only we will, then the future will be assured, and the day of brotherhood and peace will dawn.

In the final analysis, if we believe the foregoing, it doesn't make any difference whether we believe in a God at all or not. We need just to be genuinely enough devoted to the common human ideals to eliminate race prejudice, to establish democratic government, to combat communism, or whatever other power happens to be the threat to the status quo at the moment. Besides, it is a matter of common knowledge that those bearing the Christian name have been far outstripped by atheistic humanitarians in their zeal for the underdog, the elimination of prejudice and poverty, and the reign of universal justice. We can, therefore, believe in God if we like, but this is pretty much an option that is up to us. Some people are tougher than others and can get along without the comforts of religion, but others need that stay and encouragement. The test should be pragmatic at all times: whether or not it works. A religion is true in direct proportion to whether or not it works. We must will to believe in the future or we can never materialize that future.

There are many variations on this basic theme of moral idealism mixed with pragmatic this-worldliness. At the present time, it is taking the form particularly of identification with the American way of life. (Witness, for instance, the fulminations of Norman Vincent Peale, who in the words of Reinhold Niebuhr, has reduced the gospel to a soporific for tired businessmen and a shot in the arm for aspiring ones.) Democracy and the free enterprise system are set forth as the political and economic versions of Christianity. Democracy posits the inherent rights of all men—regardless of race, sex, color, religion—to life, liberty, and the pursuit of happiness!

These "versions" of Christianity are blindly equated with the *Christian* assertion that all men are equally dependent upon the grace and love of God and that their equality is in their sinfulness and not in some worth they have to God or in and of themselves. Before God, man has no rights, he has only obligations; the rest is grace. Man is created out of love and given all his gifts and talents without any merit or worthiness in him. There is no warrant for identifying democracy, and particularly our version of it, with Christianity. This is simply making Christianity the defender of the status quo, as has usually been the case, instead of allowing it to sit in judgment on all our human achievements.

Likewise with the free enterprise system. This system can be identified easily enough with a certain kind of moral idealism which believes that virtue is rewarded and that initiative, thrift, and obedience in general to the laws of fair play make for general well-being and prosperity. Likewise, it can be identified with that idealism which believes that there is a fairy godmother watching over the affairs of men who sees to it that the selfishness of men is always curbed for the good of all. Forceful restraints upon individual aggressiveness are, therefore, not necessary. The less control, the better for all concerned, for a man's own enlightened self-interest will set the necessary restraints, and the laws of the universe themselves will regulate the healthy flow of supply and demand. Such fatuous idealism is equated with faith in the power and rule of a good God. There is no radical evil; all works out for the best, because of the structure of the universe. So, again, God can go begging, because the clock he has made runs in accordance with its own laws, which of course God himself cannot change if his watch is to keep time.

FASCISM

In National Socialism (German style) and Fascism (Italian style), the world has witnessed the inevitable reaction to an over-optimistic moral idealism and the failure of the church to be true to the full dimensions of the revelation entrusted to it. Community under the conditions of existence depends upon the right balance between the role of authority and the freedom of the individual. Democracy depends for its successful working upon the intelligence, the inner moral restraints, and the capacity for self-government of the individual members of the group. When these are lacking, a strong arm takes over, and, in the interests of general security and order, the freedom of the individual is sacrificed. The whole culture as described in previous chapters, lacking both the inner restraints and the cohesive structures which once helped to stabilize it, was ripe for a cult of blood and soil, of force and will to power. The result was the monster of the totalitarian state, which brought into play demonic forces which a civilized world was believed to have outgrown.

Fascism takes its name from the Roman symbol of authority, a bundle of rods bound together with a projecting ax. Its main features are absolute national unity and absolute centralization of authority. It has its spiritual ancestors in Machiavelli and the pragmatists. Machiavelli's prince is the prototype of Il Duce and the Fuehrer. The prince may do anything to get power and to maintain it. No stratagem, no artifice, no deceit, no treachery are denied him, if only they consolidate and conserve his power. The key word is action; the end justifies the means; if a thing works it is true. In an intolerable situation of chaos the strong leader usurps power, and whatever he can make work in order to restore order and insure security is for the moment right.

All forms of fascism betray the same general features: (1) an ultranationalism (the cult of blood and soil), coupled with intolerance against minority groups within and aggressiveness without in foreign affairs; (2) a social and economic order which maintains private property and the traditional class structure in such a way, however, that all managers and owners are forced to make their decisions to serve the ends of the state; (3) an authoritarian organization of the most radical kind with power centralized in a pseudocharismatic "leader" who manipulates people instead of induing them with grace, and whose power is uncurbed by either a parliament, cabinet, constitution, or the courts. At his beck and call is the ruling party. From it are drawn all the officers of the state; to it is assigned the task of supervising all activities so that no one escapes this scrutiny; it must be the source of cultural inspiration and must "generate anew the ideological energies." To it is also entrusted the supreme defense of the regime. Whatever show of democracy is combined with this is purely ceremonial; (4) a scheme of managed culture always in the service of the state from which no area of life is excluded: education, art, religion, recreation, etc.

From this type of organization stem all the familiar totalitarian abuses: the loss of all the cherished liberties, freedom of speech, of the press, of religion, the right of trial by jury and to be confronted by one's accusers, etc. The individual has no rights which cannot be arbitrarily confiscated. Thus all freedom is bartered for a specious security.[9]

It may seem as though this kind of fascism no longer is a threat today. This would, however, be a disastrous misunderstanding, for fascism is not only the specific political structure described above. It is a demonic spirit that may take hold of any people whenever their basic security is threatened. The powerful nation, no less than the underdog, may fall its victim. The underdog nation in its struggle for power makes for itself unwarranted pretensions, and so becomes frantic and stops at nothing to attain status; while the powerful nation, never quite sure of itself either, is always seeking to bolster its position. Fascism always appears under the guise of patriotism, but in reality it is the abuse of the power of government to serve the interests of a few supposedly superior people. It has its own subtle ways of insinuating itself into power, so that before you know it you are sold out. Jingoistic nationalism of all kinds, race pride and color prejudice, the resort to political power to advance one part of the nation over another or arbitrarily to restrict the rights of certain elements of the population in contrast to others, all betray incipient fascism. In McCarthyism, we had a brilliant example of the temper and the tactics of fascism ruthlessly trampling on all human rights and offending human dignity. As previous chapters have shown, the modern, uprooted mass man is easy prey for the fascist leader who promises security. The mass media of propaganda are all at his disposal; the emotions are easily aroused; a sudden well-planned coup d'état could not fail of success. In fact, to what extent we are already unwitting victims of fascist thought control is a matter of grave concern.

In such a state of affairs the Christian church has something

[9] For the above see *The Annals of the American Academy of Political Science:* "Socialism, Fascism, and Democracy," CLXXX (July, 1935), especially pp. 9 ff., pp. 47 ff., pp. 55 ff., pp. 62 ff.; N. S. Timasheff, *Three Worlds* (Milwaukee: Bruce Publishing Co., 1946).

to say. Eivind Berggrav, speaking directly out of the experience of Nazi oppression, points out that there is no real curb to the power of the totalitarian state except that which comes from within man himself.[10] But this protest from within must have a genuinely transcendent source. Autonomous man who is a law unto himself cannot stand up against heteronomy. Natural law which is severed from a living God soon loses its authority. The law and the state should be surrounded with an aura of holiness which inspires with proper awe and respect. God alone, however, is the Holy One, and to him alone is due the ultimate respect and awe. Whatever aura of holiness, therefore, surrounds the state does not belong to it in its own right, but only because it is divinely ordained. "The powers that be are ordained of God" (Rom. 13:1). When the living God is no longer worshiped, then ideologies take his place and the state itself is deified. There remains no court of appeal to which men can turn to protest the totalitarian demands of the state. There is, therefore, no safeguard against the tyranny of the state except in a genuinely transcendent God. An "immanent mystic" humanism offers no really transcendent hold.

Fascism is a false hope and the church must witness against it. The church must show that the state is one of God's structures of creation given in love to a sinful world. The state is equipped with the power of the sword to punish the evildoer and reward the righteous. The state must, therefore, be confined to its proper God-given task in the keeping of order and the administration of justice, but must not itself be allowed to usurp all functions. This is a violation of God's order which is destructive of community. Under the protection of the state, the church must retain the freedom of criticism. In the totalitarian state, the question arises, "Quis custodiet ipsos custodes?" When not only all the power of government—legislative, executive, judicial

[10] Eivind Berggrav, *Man and State* (Philadelphia: Muhlenberg Press, 1951).

—but all other aspects of life, education, art, religion, recreation, etc., are concentrated in the same hands, "Who then is to guard the guardians?" Without setting it up as beyond criticism, the American system may nevertheless be cited over against totalitarianism for its realistic system of checks and balances which reflect its mistrust of the innate goodness of man by preventing a concentration of power in a few hands. It is this system, as just conceived, which is now in jeopardy, and the Christian church has something to say about it that is relevant.

COMMUNISM—"THE GOD THAT FAILED"

"Communism is the belief that society can be altered by turning men into machines for altering society." [11]

Communism has been called a Christian heresy. Every heresy is an indictment of the church, since it always fastens itself on one of the church's weaknesses. Communism developed, in part at least, in protest to the gross evils of society the church was powerless to alleviate. It also fastened on certain aspects of theological orthodoxy and of liberalism which played into its hands.

So, for example, a theology which divides man into body and soul and makes the church's sole concern the salvation of the soul in an escape from an evil material world, to the neglect of the resurrection of the body and the redemption of the whole creation in a new heaven and a new earth, opens itself up for the communist ideological distortion. When theology forgets that a new age has already dawned and that the whole creation is moving toward its consummation and that true community and right living together are, within the limitations of sinfulness and finitude, a real possibility on the earth and not just a recollection of a lost paradise, then the Communist takes over with his fantastic determination to make community a reality.

[11] Stephen Spender, in *The God That Failed*, ed. R. H. Crossman (New York: Bantam Books, 1952), p. 275.

On the other hand, when theology loses its tragic sense of life and does not take seriously that the consummation lies beyond the end of history, that this is to the very end a time of struggle and decision, that this is the time of crisis in which at any moment man may by the wrong decision come into the power of Satan, that there is no guarantee of evolutionary progress, that true community must be daily restored by the renewal of the God-relation in contrition and faith, then again communism takes over with its falsely and disastrously optimistic view of a determined process of nature bound inevitably to reach its goal.

If one thing is clear, it is that communism is itself a religion. To be a Communist demands an absolute loyalty such as only God would have the right to claim from any man. Communism is not only a *Weltanschauung*, (world view), but an all-engrossing, all-encompassing loyalty. It demands not only intellectual assent to certain dogmas, but above all it demands obedience, which is the essence of religion. It means a transformation of existence so that life is seen with other eyes and all values become transformed. It is something that must be lived. So, communism can teach men again that Christianity must also be an "existential communication," when to man, in his existence, there is communicated the mind and will of Jesus Christ.

It is sometimes said that it is necessary to distinguish between communism as an economic theory and communism as an all-inclusive world view and a religious faith. It is sometimes further suggested that the church cannot rightly quarrel with communism as an economic theory, because that lies outside of its sphere of competence. Of course, there are non-Marxist socialist views of all kinds. These will all have to be judged on their own merits and are not under consideration now. We are dealing now with that communism which we know to be a militant, crusading religion, bidding for world dominion today, and which is not at all merely an economic theory for economists alone to judge. It is not a question of whether or not communism can serve the

Russians best so that they can be left to stew in their own juice, while communism itself is dedicated to world revolution.

Regardless of the fact that no nation today can be isolated from the rest of the world, it is the central claim of communism that the very thing preventing the Utopia they promise is the capitalist encirclement. It is not only its thesis that this encirclement must end before there can be world peace and universal prosperity, but it is also its thesis, supposedly based on accurate and scientific knowledge, that this encirclement will end with the same certainty that an explosion occurs after lighting a fuse—nay, with greater certainty, for there is no possibility of any upsetting turn of fate or the intervention of any god. The present change of tactics and the Stalin debunking phase does not alter these basic tenets one bit. In fact—until there is much more evidence to the contrary than there is at present—it only supports the contention that every opportunity is to be exploited to achieve the inevitable end. To drop one's guard at this point would be fatal.

This is not something which the church can ignore. It is something which no man, no organization and no cult or creed can ignore, because the cult of communism cries the lie to every other claim to truth. Here is a view that at last makes clear the necessity of a decisive "either-or." *You cannot be both a committed Communist and a committed Christian.* This claim of communism to have the right answer, precisely in matters of ultimate concern as well as in peripheral matters, this claim upon the loyalty and the obedience, the thoughts and aspirations of men the world around, this bid for the souls of men may not be that of *the* Antichrist, but it certainly is anti-Christian, and it must be answered by the church. It is destructive of community, of life-together-in-love. It is a false hope which must be answered by the gospel.

There are many competent analyses of communism which show its anti-Christian character and make clear that the Christian cannot compromise with it.[12] It is our purpose here only to point out those elements which underlie the conviction that this is indeed a false hope.

Communism asserts that the whole course of history is predetermined and will necessarily run its course to the realization of a classless society in which all shall contribute according to their ability, and all shall share in accordance with their need. As is well known, Marx took the Hegelian dialectic and turned it upside down. Instead of the course of history being the unfolding of the divine mind from above, it is driven by the material factor from below. Underlying and involved in this view of history is the following: All things are constituted by their relations, and there is nothing permanently stable in the universe. There are no indivisible atoms which constitute the building stones of the universe. Above all there are no individual human beings everlastingly riveted fast to themselves. They, too, are constituted by their relations and just as the elements that make up water dissolve to form other compounds, so will these elements that compose man. At death, therefore, man dissolves into his component parts and is no more. And during his lifetime man changes his disposition in accordance with his relations, which are nothing but material relationships. This has close kinship with the analysis of existence given above (see page 121), with the all-important difference that the God-relationship to man as a center of responsibility has been omitted. It is due entirely to material relations that a man is greedy, power-hungry, lustful, deceitful, destroying himself and others, while if these material relations are changed, he loses these traits and becomes a paragon of virtue.

The fall of man, the alienation or estrangement, is not man's

[12] See the bibliography and especially the articles in the *Christian Century*: John Bennett, "Can We Ever Support Communism?" (June 11, 1952), pp. 696 ff., and Karl Barth, "Letter to Bishop Bereczky" (July 30, 1952), pp. 876 ff. Also *The Lutheran* for December 3, 1952 and January 7, 1953: Bishop Dibelius on the situation in East Germany.

proud rebellion against his maker which really severs the bond of love with the neighbor, but it is the original division of labor and the subsequent beginning of the class struggle. By separating man from his work, by creating an antithesis between manual and intellectual labor, men are set against each other. Now history repeatedly marches from thesis to antithesis to synthesis until the proper synthesis is finally achieved. Capitalism has within it the seeds of its own dissolution. Through world revolution and the subsequent dictatorship of the proletariat, during which the state will gradually wither away, the classless society will come into being. Then when the relations which constitute man are properly adjusted, all inequalities and injustices will disappear. (This is the counterpart to the Christian reconciliation when men by being brought into the right God-relationship are also brought into the right relationship to each other.)

There are thus no essential differences between individuals such as male and female, and ruler and ruled, and no differences resulting from special capacities which lead to a division of labor in the economic sphere. In the classless society of the future, Marx has everyone doing whatever he turns his fancy to, building a bridge in the morning, composing a sonata in the afternoon, and spending his evenings smoking an excellent cigar. Here then is a self-sufficient individual, independent of the brother. This cuts to the heart of community.

In the interim period leading up to this golden age, however, everything is different. Now there must be coercion, each person must be fitted forcibly to his niche, and there are no standards or values whatsoever except those which further the end. As with Machiavelli's prince, anything goes: lies, intrigue, violence—anything that promotes the cause. If there is complaint about the millions who are sacrificed by these means, then the finger of scorn is pointed at the many millions who are at present succumbing to plagues and wars and other catastrophes simply because of man's inadequate planning or co-operation in making available to all the benefits of science. At least the casualties of the Soviets are not left to chance! They are deliberately planned to further the end. Besides, there is nothing man can do about it anyway. All these things are bound to happen. The only freedom a man can possibly have is the recognition of his "unfreedom," and if he gives himself unstintingly to the cause, he will at least have the assurance that he is not an obstructionist. Thus history is on the march and the glorious tomorrow is a certainty. Though none today shall share it, they shall have the satisfaction of having furthered it.

How desperately committed the Communists are is tellingly revealed in an incident told by Arthur Koestler in *Darkness at Noon*. The former Soviet leader is on trial for his life because he has grown soft in his efforts to bring about the great day of liberation. His torturer reminds him of how horrified a delegation of English women had been when inspecting one of the factories because the workers who were late or who fell asleep at their monotonous machine jobs were accused of sabotage and without any kind of fair trial were either sent to the salt mines or liquidated then and there. In justification of this action the Inquisitor asks the accused how old he had been when he had first come into possession of a watch. He answers that he may have been a boy of nine or ten. Whereupon his torturer says that he, as a peasant boy, had never even seen a watch until he was sixteen years old. He tells of how the peasants would go to the railroad station and wait for the train. Perhaps it came at noon, perhaps at night, perhaps not until the next day. What was the difference? Time meant nothing to them. And now those same peasants are under the Five Year Plan, they are catching the commuters' train and punching a time clock. In a few years they have had to make up for thousands of years of slow development and have had to be made over into the time-conscious, wrist watch-consulting, brunch-gulping creatures that are bringing in the millennium on their grease-stained shirt tails. If they are late, there is no virtue in softness. It makes no sense to take circumstances into account.

What matters is not the present but the future. In fact "Soviet realism" treats the past as though it did not exist and the future as though it had already arrived, while "bourgeois formalism" means an "excessive loyalty to facts instead of hopes." What matters is not the well-being of these few peasants, but the well-being of the totality in the future! So you have to crack the whip, that is to say, the machine gun. Whatever clogs up the machinery must be gotten rid of—or how shall you ever usher in the golden age? This incident sums up better than many a page of theoretical discussion the orthodox Communist ideology. Every other previous attempt at bettering the human situation has failed because men turned squeamish. This one will not fail because there will be no squeamishness.

With such a system there is no possibility of compromise. In its striving for community it destroys the individual, because there is, in the first place, no individual who is a center of responsibility before God. Moreover, underneath there is the same confusion which has prevailed since the days of the Enlightenment and which has been the ruling assumption of capitalism. Instead of love—i.e., suprarational love in the sense of *agape*—reason is made the highest arbiter, and then it is assumed that reason will guide men into community by showing them where their best interests lie.[13] Autonomous man's reason is by itself believed able to figure out the ends of life and to dictate the terms of community. Paradoxically enough, Marxism is a reasoned world view which believes that it has the scientific evidence on its side. While it can be refuted in part on scientific and reasonable grounds, the final refutation must come from the standpoint of revelation which shows how communism's understanding of man and of community, of the source of evil, and of

[13] See Eduard Heimann, "A Christian Looks at Communism" in *The Christian Demand for Social Justice*, ed. Bishop Scarlett (New York: New American Library, 1949).

the whole meaning of the course of history, are all basically distorted.

The non-Christian who does not have his eyes blinded by the communist ideology can see clearly enough from our whole Western heritage that the transfer of property from private to public hands is in itself no solution and must mean, if radically carried through, an infringement upon personal dignity and liberty. He can see that "the world needs . . . a balance of economic and political powers so that no party, no class, no government, no assembly of private interests is omnipotent and beyond challenge," and that "Soviet Russia lacks this balance." [14] He can see that it is disastrous when the government itself usurps all functions and does not observe a proper division of labor, not allowing the various forms of community (the family, the economic order, the various cultural orders) to perform their free function.

The non-Christian can see that there must be guardians to guard the guardians and that there was wisdom in our founding fathers' keeping the judiciary separate from the legislative and executive branches of the government. (Our founders recognized the sinful propensities of men when they set up the necessary safeguards to the pride of power.) He can see that there must be "full liberty to dissenters and to those of contrasting religions, races, appearances, name. . . ." [15] He can see that there must be an internationalism which excludes jingoistic nationalism and at the same time allows room for national freedom and individuality just as allowances are made for the individual in the community. He can see that there must always be respect for the human being and that all social institutions exist only for the welfare and the development of the human being. It is not necessary to be a Christian to see all this.

[14] Louis Fischer, in *The God That Failed*, ed. R. H. Crossman (New York: Bantam Books, 1952), pp. 229 ff.
[15] *Ibid*, pp. 229 ff.

But what the non-Christian, apart from revelation, does not have is a recognition of what it really means to be a human being who is called by God from eternity to respond to the word of love; who nevertheless does not respond in this way spontaneously; and who, therefore, needs to be born again. What man needs is God's approach to him in unconditional forgiveness. What he needs is justification by grace alone, in order that this may break his pride and so set for him the pattern of true communiy. Therefore, it is with the specifically Christian categories that communism is to be met, and not with the universally humane religiosity that cannot deal realistically with the human situation.

ROMAN CATHOLICISM—"A THEOLOGY OF GLORY"

It is with reservations that Roman Catholicism is here branded as a false hope. Everything is said in the spirit of love, not in order to antagonize and divide still further, but in order to draw together those who acknowledge the absolute lordship of Christ and are intent only upon doing his will. An ecumenical movement which exists only for the purpose of drawing the "Prots" together in order to bludgeon Roman Catholics would be a sorry spectacle of ecumenicity. In reply to Roman Catholic insistence that there can be no solution of the existing divisions except by a return to Mother Church, the Protestant viewpoint must be made clear that there is no argument about the fact that the church is the mother of us all and that, humanly speaking, there is no salvation outside of the church. It all depends, however, on the definition of the church.

Karl Adam is right when he says that Luther by no means meant to separate the Protestants from the church.[16] Yet Adam does not seem to penetrate to the depths of Luther's conception of the church as the communion of saints, i.e., of those who are Christs to each other. Adam is also right, in a sense, when he says

[16] See Karl Adam, *One and Holy* (New York: Sheed and Ward, 1951).

that it was Luther's Occamism which kept him from finding the peace that he craved and that he would have found it in the Thomistic system, where the initial guarantees are given by the reason so that revelation need only build on them. This gives an initial rational certainty of God's existence and of the basic virtues and does not leave one at the mercy of a capricious God who does only what he wills.

Luther did indeed follow Occam, in that he would "let God be God." [17] God dictates his own terms and the *deus revelatus* remains the *deus absconditus*. Therefore, the only assurance a man can have of salvation is, as Luther put it, in the Word. But this does not mean, as it has come to mean for most Protestants, just the Bible. It means the living Christ. No insight of the reason, no external hierarchy of priests, no "paper pope," no system of theology, can take the place of this apprehension by the living Christ. Luther's fulminations against the "whore of reason" and the "Babylonian Captivity" of the church are to be understood in the light of his belief that they usurped the sole authority and the honor of Christ and that they constituted idolatry by putting a human authority in the place of God. God himself in Christ, through the power of the Holy Spirit, must give the assurance of salvation. That is why the Word is always primary, even in relation to the sacraments, lest these become idols also.

What is the "Babylonian Captivity" but bondage to a false overlord? Neither in autonomy nor in heteronomy but only in theonomy is there true freedom. The assurance of salvation and the release from the desperation that drove Luther to his excesses is to be found only in the sovereign love of God which goes *contra rationem* (contrary to reason) and *contra legem* (contrary to the law) and forgives unconditionally. Assurance of salvation rests on God-engendered faith and not on some kind of external guarantees such as the hierarchy means to provide. God's love

[17] See Philip Watson, *Let God Be God* (Philadelphia: Muhlenberg Press, 1948).

alone is absolute and supreme and needs no sort of bolstering or defense. How can God's love be judged when it itself judges everything? How can it be defended when it itself must break down all defenses? Such love needs no supplementation, neither from good works, nor from arguments, nor from any man-made machinations. It is from this love that the good works flow, and it is this love which takes captive the reason and whispers into her ear the most persuasive arguments on behalf of the beloved, just as any lover cannot cease to sing the praises of his love and to give a thousand reasons why she and she alone is the queen of heaven.

It is this sovereign love alone which can set men free for service and so build true community. A man is accepted by God unconditionally and he is not used by God to fulfil in God some need or longing. God loves man for himself alone. Just so must a man love his neighbor; so must he serve him. As long as a man is working out his salvation by good works, he will inevitably "use" his neighbor; his neighbor becomes the tool to his satisfaction, the ladder by means of which he climbs up into heaven, and so the very nerve of true community is cut. The absolute which sits in judgment on all men's efforts to build community is relativized. The selfishness which eats into the heart of the most intimate human relationships has found its justification and been sanctified with its aura of holiness. No matter how many genuine Roman Catholic saints there may be who, like St. Francis Xavier, give expression to the deepest longing of their heart by saying,

> Not for the hope of glory or reward,
> But even as Thyself hast loved me, Lord,
> I love Thee, and will love Thee and adore,
> Who art my King, my God, for evermore.[18]

---

[18] *Common Service Book,* Board of Publication, United Lutheran Church in America, Philadelphia, Pa., Hymn No. 58.

there is that in the Roman Catholic system of work-right-eousness which destroys true community and which must be purged before the true gospel can shine forth. These criticisms are directed, therefore, against the basic structure of the Roman Catholic hierarchical system, because it is believed to be destructive of freedom and true community, and because it substitutes a theology of glory for a theology of the cross.

Apparently many are ripe today for a return to the sheltering womb of Mother Church. For the victim of meaninglessness and homelessness, there is the great, solid, impregnable rock of the church. In its priesthood, in the structure of its hierarchy, it has visible continuity against the flux of time. In the ever-recurring miracle of the Mass, which the church alone controls, there is the guarantee of God's entry into human life and his doing something for man's redemption. Ever and again, in the inspired phrase of Bruce Marshall, "Christ comes again through the morning in the swift, white sacrament of love." The tabernacle on the altar is the tabernacle of God among men, thus anticipating the promise of the Apocalypse. When the Host is paraded in the monstrance, this is like the ark of the covenant of old, God's presence among his people. The aura of holiness is here and not over the state or some human figure. This is the "presence" that cannot be violated with immunity. This is the *mysterium tremendum*, the *mysterium fascinans*, that both attracts and repels and holds you spellbound, wanting to flee yet rooted to the ground, the earthly element transubstantiated into the divine.

The church also has its intellectual appeal, in addition to the appeal of its mysticism. It has clear specific answers that are grounded in the reason given to every man. In Koestler's *Age of Longing*, the little French nun explains to the groping novice:

The contemplation—the meditation—the mystic sentiment—you think that is all one needs. But the sentiment is liquid—now it fills you, now it runs out of you through a puncture made by a small, sharp temptation, a little sin, an ugliness like the prick of a needle. You are in peace, you are perhaps in a state of grace—of friendship with God, as we say—and then there is that little puncture, this laceration, and the peace is finished, the grace is finished, the sentiment runs out—glub, glub—you are left empty and dry. But there is this pond, there are the water lilies, it is also liquid, but why is it always full and still? Because the pond is held together by its banks, by limitations with a hard and definite form. Without these limitations, the rigid dogmatism of the banks, the liquid could not keep its fulness and stillness. *Voila* ... There is a price to pay for this peace. It is surrender ... *Il n'y a que le premiere pas qui coute*—the rest must follow by itself, as you will see.[19]

The intellectual appeal is in the rigid system of dogmas that beam their certainty like a lighthouse through the storm. They have been fixed once and for all. The Latin language, as a dead language, is the bearer of these fixed dogmas. The Aristotelian categories provide the framework for all time. Morality is code morality which tries to evade the tragic conflicts of duties. Conduct is governed by an immense system of casuistry worked out to the minutest detail. There is no freedom for the following of the divine imperative of love in each situation.

It is believed, of course, that there is provision enough for growth and development provided by tradition and the constant guidance of the Holy Spirit. The doctrine of the pope's infallibility whenever he speaks ex cathedra is not as crude as sometimes supposed. The pope's final dictum comes only at the end of a long chain of development and after the most careful investigation. Nevertheless, this sort of dependence upon the church is an infringement upon the freedom of the individual. It is a surrender of freedom for the sake of security. It is one of the aspects of a theology of glory instead of a theology of the cross. A rigid system of dogma and a code morality, even if allowance be made for change and development, is something quite different from the maintenance of the circle of revelation and faith within

[19] Arthur Koestler, *The Age of Longing* (New York: Macmillan Co., 1951), pp. 50-51.

which the Christian moves. In maintaining this circle, the individual does give up his autonomy, but he does not give it up to another human being; he does not simply believe what the priest tells him to believe and do what the priest tells him to do, but he gives up his autonomy for a genuine theonomy, the rule of God in his life.

There is that in Roman Catholicism which would seem to make it first of all a religion and not a philosophy. It is based on event and encounter. It is based upon the events of history when God at a specific time and place encountered men, and this event and encounter are constantly repeated at a time and place. The church is not a lecture hall, but it is the temple of God's presence and activity. The priest is not a professor, but a mediator between God and man, bridging the gap of rebellion and sin. He also has a prophetic voice and derives his authority, not from the inspiration of genius, but from a sure "thus saith the Lord." Yet there is a confusion of categories involved. Underneath there is a succumbing to the pride of the intellect and of morals and of power. Those solid dogmatisms, which keep the waters from seeping off into the arid sands, are a bulwark against being thrown entirely upon God. The categories are not the dynamic categories of the Bible.

This may be briefly demonstrated, first, in the Roman Catholic concept of grace. Grace is viewed as a power infused and not as the disposition of God in love and unconditional forgiveness. This paves the way for the whole Roman Catholic system. To be sure, the part that man plays is reduced to an irreducible minimum, but that minimum remains. Man makes only the first motion (*si homo facit quod in se est*—if a man does what it is in him to do). Even this first motion may be ascribed to God by indirection, since he made man in his image. Nevertheless, it is man's initial motion. Then, in response to this initial impetus of man, God injects a "shot" of grace, in the strength of which a man must perform a good work if the grace is not to be so much power wasted. This is faith active in love. Each good work performed in the strength of God's grace merits another injection of grace, and so on. This is a quantitatively computable matter, so that it is possible finally to accumulate supererogatory works which go into the treasury on which others may draw. A man's salvation may then be said to be entirely a work of grace.

The difference between this view of grace and the evangelical view should be made clear. The Roman view can be compared with a ladder, which is first let down from above and upon which man then must make the laborious ascent in the strength that God supplies. Jacob's ladder, however, brought the presence of God down to sinful, scheming Jacob and it was midst the anxieties of his human, sinful situation that Jacob experienced that presence.

The whole Roman Catholic sacramental system hinges on its conception of grace. The priest, in virtue of his valid ordination, alone has the power to call Christ down in the Mass; he alone can perform a valid sacrament and so mediate the grace of God to man. All mankind, therefore, becomes dependent upon the church and its priests in a different way than the way in which all men are dependent for their redemption upon the proclamation of the gospel and the presence of Christ in the Word. The church has been compared to a giant oil monopoly with the priests in charge of the pipe lines.[20] It seems nothing short of a survival of paganism, where the priests, in virtue of their esoteric powers, transmitted to them externally and *ex opere operato*, keep their hold upon men. To such extremes is this power of the priest carried. He requires no learning whatsoever, if only he stands in the succession and has voice enough to intone the liturgy. (This is, of course, other than saying that all that is necessary is the actual proclamation of the gospel, which is unaffected by the learning or the character of the one who proclaims it.) In every

[20] See Karl Heim, *Spirit and Truth: the Nature of Evangelical Christianity* (London: Lutterworth Press, 1935).

crisis of life, man is dependent upon the ministrations of the church. If he is not married by the priest, he is living in adultery; if the priest does not accompany him on his last journey, he gets off to a very bad start in purgatory.

The same quantitative aspect is dominant in the Mass. The sacrifice of the Mass becomes quantitatively computable and applicable. The number of the Masses determines the flow of grace, like the turning on of so many spigots. No amount of theoretical apologetic can offset what is actually done in practice in this respect, where Masses are bought and paid for and applied quantitatively to both the living and the dead. No true community can possibly be built on the basis of such a vast system of barter. What you could get out of it, of course, is a neat defense of capitalism and the profit motive. The competitive scramble would only reflect what goes on at the heavenly bargain tables.

In the theory of transubstantiation, particularly, the static category of substance replaces a real, dynamic, personal presence. This theory also reflects the quantitative conception of the flow of grace. Instead of its being a person present, it is a substance that flows. The Aristotelian distinction between substance and accidents explains the mystery of the sacrament. While the accidents remain the same, the substance is changed. This substance, the glorified blood, must be most carefully guarded; every drop must be washed from the chalice; when it is spilled it must be licked from the stones. Here it becomes clear how man applies the categories of the reason, and forces the mystery of the really miraculous coming of God into the flesh into this human mould. A quantitatively controllable substance takes the place of the living God with his disposition of love and grace toward men.

The same quantitative substantial conception is reflected also in the Roman Catholic view of man. Man is conceived as a substance which can be gradually and quantitatively transformed, like the gradual transformation of muddy water into clear water by means of a sufficient number of transfusions. Man must not first *be* good in his inmost disposition, before he can *do* good, as is clear from Jesus' parable, "Do men gather grapes of thorns, or figs of thistles?" Instead, a man, as Aristotle said, *becomes good by doing good*. The Christian, thus, is not the reborn man constantly in struggle with the old Adam and always on the way toward realizing the purpose for which he was made, but never realizing that purpose. It is obscured that a man is actually constituted by his relations, primarily the relation of faith which needs constantly to be renewed and which never, like knowledge, becomes a permanent possession which will some day give way to sight. Instead, man is a substance in process of being purged by repeated infusions of grace. Process thus really replaces crisis and decision. A man is thus dependent upon the sacramental powers of the church, and he can never really attain to the certainty of salvation which rests upon the all-sufficiency of God's love.

The final and inclusive indictment of the Roman Catholic church is that it has substituted a theology of glory for the theology of the cross. This means that the servant form of the church is really denied and its hiddenness is violated. Everywhere —in the outward structure of the church with its direct apostolic succession, in its claim to disposable power and absolute authority, in its outward splendor and pageantry—there is the denial of the servant form and the hiddenness of the true church which makes salvation rest upon faith alone. As Dostoevski means to show in his legend of The Grand Inquisitor in *The Brothers Karamazov*,[21] they have corrected Christ's work. Christ withstood the temptations of the dread spirit in the wilderness, but they have listened to the voice of the tempter; they have grown impatient of the terrific price of freedom in much the same way as the com-

[21] See Feodor Dostoevski, *The Brothers Karamazov* (New York: Modern Library, Random House, 1950), pp. 292 ff.

153

munists. The people are like sheep without a shepherd and they need to be herded to the stalls. A nadir of need is apparent when men will choose security instead of freedom. Because men are incapable of freedom, they must be overwhelmed with miracles and mystery and authority. The church must exercise its rule for the good of men, and instead of its being the servant, it must be the ruler.

The Roman Catholic church has never given up its ideal of being in the dominant position, not only through the power of its proclamation, but actually in the organization of its hierarchy. It is one thing to say that the gospel must sit in judgment upon all human achievements and that all earthly powers and governments are under its dominion. It is an altogether different thing to give this place to the hierarchy in which the true church loses its hiddenness and becomes identified with a transubstantiated, ordained priesthood. It is at this point that the priesthood becomes most destructive of community. The evangelical conception of the universal priesthood means that every Christian is to be a priest, serving his neighbor with the gospel of love, speaking to him the Word of forgiveness, opening to him his own heart and accepting the other as a brother just as he is, in his sin, even as Jesus did when he walked among men. It is this living of the gospel of forgiveness which alone can establish community in the family and in the other human relations, and not the dispensing of oil by those who have the monopoly of it. To be sure, Christians alone have the gospel, the Word of God's love, and this gospel must be released to open men to each other and transform aggregates into communities, but this is different from making everyone dependent upon the hierarchy.

Mother Church has an ample bosom at which she nourishes many children. She takes care to make room for everyone. She takes every superstition and every philosophy and somehow gives it a home, and so she seems to be the answer to all men's search. She certainly also shelters many in whom the love of

God is incarnate. Nevertheless, there is a spirit of Catholicism, and there is another spirit of evangelical Christianity. In evangelical Christianity the one, holy, catholic, apostolic church is the mother. This church was born on Pentecost with the sending of the Spirit, and it spreads from place to place only as it is proclaimed from Jerusalem through Judea and Samaria to the uttermost parts of the earth. This church is bound to the means of grace, the proclaimed Word and the Word become visible and active in the sacraments. This Word, whether in the form of proclamation or of sacramental action, is never anything other than the living Lord of the church as he addresses and transforms his children. The church is not a lecture hall and pastors are not professors. They are stewards of the mysteries of God.

There is a proclamation of the gospel which can give men—if they will receive it—their proper dignity and worth, the full security of everlasting salvation, and fellowship with the living God and his communion of saints. There is a proclamation of the gospel which means to leaven society from within and to preserve it from corruption. There is an authority of the Spirit which is the only true freedom and which avoids the pitfalls of totalitarianism, whether in the state or in the church. There is a Protestant spirit which refuses to fixate at any level of human inerpretation, but is always open to the present speaking of God. There is an evangelical spirit which will obey the divine imperative anew in each situation in such a way that love becomes the divine indicative: "We love because he first loved us" (I John 4:19). In the ecumenical church there is a growing unanimity about that gospel which is the answer to man's restless search. It is to that we must turn.

BIBLIOGRAPHY

An Analysis of the Present Situation:

Kierkegaard, S. *The Present Age.* New York: Oxford Univ. Press, 1940.

In this prophetic little book, Kierkegaard describes the mass man who has ceased to be an individual before the living God, but is shaped by the "public."

Kierkegaard, S. *The Sickness Unto Death.* Princeton: Princeton Univ. Press, 1941.

Here Kierkegaard gives his analysis of existence, of selfhood, and of the various forms of despair possessing those not grounded in faith in the true source of their being.

Atheistic Existentialism:

Sartre, Jean Paul. *Existentialism.* New York: Philosophical Library, 1947.

In very brief compass, Sartre clearly states the basis of his humanism in a world in which there is no god and man is free, within the bounds of the given, to make himself whatever he wills.

The Christianity of Main Street:

Wedel, Theodore. *The Christianity of Main Street.* New York: Macmillan Co., 1950.

This is a careful appraisal of the average American's conception of Christianity, both in and out of the churches, which gives a clue to the present day return to religion of the Norman Vincent Peale variety.

Fascism:

Berggrav, Eivind. *Man and State.* Philadelphia: Muhlenberg Press, 1951.

Coming as it did out of the fires of oppression, this is a most valuable discussion of the relation between church and state and the rights of the individual under the state from the Christian point of view. It corrects current misunderstandings of Luther's concept of authority.

Also valuable in this connection are:

Carlson, Edgar M. *The Church and the Public Conscience.* Philadelphia: Muhlenberg Press, 1956.

Ruff, G. Elson. *The Dilemma of Church and State.* Philadelphia: Muhlenberg Press, 1954.

Communism:

Bennett, J. C. *Christianity and Communism*. New York: Association Press, 1948.

Crossman, Richard (ed.). *The God That Failed*. New York: Bantam Books, 1952.

Particularly valuable because in it a group of disillusioned fellow-travelers reveal Communism's demonic delusion.

Miller, Alexander. *The Christian Significance of Karl Marx*. New York: Macmillan Co., 1947.

The books by Bennett and Miller have been selected from a wealth of material because they present simply and forcefully both the attraction and the demonic delusion of Communism.

Roman Catholicism:

Adam, Karl. *One and Holy*. New York: Sheed and Ward, Inc., 1951.

———. *The Spirit of Catholicism*. New York: Macmillan Co. 1940.

Heim, Karl. *Spirit and Truth, the Nature of Evangelical Christianity*. London: Lutterworth Press, Inc., 1935.

These two authors, read side by side, will show clearly the differences between Rome and Wittenberg. No finer apologetics for each position could be asked for; yet the differences are crucial.

INDEX

Index

Type used in this book
Body, 10 on 13 and 9 on 11 Janson
Display, Radiant and Vogue
Paper: Standard White GM Antique